D1032395

Rocky Times in Rocky Mountain National Park

Rocky Times
in Rocky Mountain National Park
AN UNNATURAL HISTORY

Karl Hess, Jr.

Senior Associate
Foundation for Research on Economics
and the Environment
Bozeman • Seattle

with a Foreword by Tom Wolf

UNIVERSITY PRESS OF COLORADO

The University Press of Colorado is a cooperative publishing enterprise supported, in part, by Adams State College, Colorado State University, Fort Lewis College, Mesa State College, Metropolitan State College of Denver, University of Colorado, University of Northern Colorado, University of Southern Colorado, and Western State College of Colorado.

Library of Congress Cataloging-in-Publication Data

Hess, Karl, 1947–
  Rocky times in Rocky Mountain National Park: an unnatural history / Karl Hess, Jr.; with a foreword by Tom Wolf.
      p.   cm.
  Includes bibliographical references (p.   ) and index.
  ISBN 0-87081-309-9
  1. Nature conservation — Colorado — Rocky Mountain National Park.   2. Rocky Mountain National Park (Colo.) — Management.   3. Ecology — Park (Colo.) — History.   I. Title.
  QH76.5.C6H47 1993
  333.78'3'0978869 — dc20   93-36452
                                                                  CIP

The paper used in this publication meets the minimum requirements of the American National Standard for Information Sciences—Permanence of Paper for Printed Library Materials. ANSI Z39.48–1984

∞

10 9 8 7 6 5 4 3 2 1

A thing is right when it tends to preserve the integrity, stability, and beauty of the biotic community. It is wrong when it tends otherwise.

—Aldo Leopold, *A Sand County Almanac*

Contents

Contents

Foreword

The history of the western United States is ecological history. The most recent of science's prophets, ecologists try to fit the role of the European settlers into the wide open spaces of the West. In its role as an international biosphere preserve, Rocky Mountain National Park is one of our great laboratories for that experiment, the results of which will mean life or death for whole ecosystems as well as for species.

Is—or was—Rocky Mountain ever "wide," "open," or a "space"? Such questions begin in history and ecology, but they end in morality and public policy. Moral values are always inherent in our history and our science. Ecology is no exception; it shapes our view of our place in a nature where "is" always issues into "ought."

This book helps us understand the linked history and ecology of Colorado's crown jewel. Karl Hess writes from the heart about Rocky Mountain, a place we all love. His is an informed heart, however, firmly connected to a head full of the best syntheses of contemporary ecology and history.

Just as today's ecology is mostly about "disturbance," some of Rocky Mountain's recent history is disturbing. In 1991 the National Park Service banished its own scientific research staff at Rocky Mountain. Park administrators did not like the "oughts" their own scientists had derived from decades of observation. Problems related to the management of elk and fire at Rocky Mountain have long been open secrets. But no one had the courage to speak out, and no one had the expertise to trace the history of conflicting views about Rocky Mountain's ecology. Now Karl Hess has given voice to the many conscientious ecologists, in and out of government service, who know that someone has blundered, and who feel that there is still time to right past mistakes.

Colorado historian Patricia Nelson Limerick has challenged scholars to make ecological history come of age by tying it to a specific place. I hope Professor Limerick will be as pleased as I am with Karl Hess's timely and temperate response. Government employees are no better or worse than the rest of us. As a former employee of both the Park Service and the Forest

Service, Hess knows that, and so he avoids the nasty personal attacks that characterized Alston Chase's 1985 book *Playing God in Yellowstone*. Chase's book spoiled Yellowstone's chances for an intellectually honest evaluation of the gap between Park Service science and administration, but Hess's courteous, informed dissent furthers critical thought about how we might close that gap. When the dust settles, everyone who cares about Rocky Mountain will welcome *Rocky Times'* critique of the Park Service's philosophy of "natural regulation."

I grew up within sight of Rocky Mountain, and I carried into Wild Basin a battered 1933 edition of Ruth Ashton Nelson's *Plants of Rocky Mountain National Park*. The seemingly serene and orderly natural world of that book was based on an ecology begotten by its times, which marched to the same sure, triumphant beat as a pioneering people entering a supposedly empty wilderness.

Much later, as a Colorado State University graduate student and contemporary of Dr. Hess, I would study field ecology at CSU's Pingree Park Campus, right on Rocky Mountain's northern boundary. Comparing Park Service and Forest Service management philosophies, we learned firsthand the interrelationships of fire, elk, beaver, ptarmigan, willow, and aspen. Because Rocky Mountain was a proposed wolf reintroduction site, and because its administrators had formulated an up-to-date fire policy, we assumed that Rocky Mountain would recover from its problems. Fifteen years later, with no fires, no wolves, and no real change in sight, I can only join in the chorus of people who are glad to see *Rocky Times*.

Only barbarians lack curiosity about where they come from and where they are going. Ecologists working in Colorado look to Rocky Mountain as a great touchstone, a place where "deliberate restraint" ought to be our guide, as CSU philosopher Holmes Rolston reminds us. But the emphasis ought to fall on both terms. In the case of elk and fire, doing nothing definitely means doing something—something terrible for the well-being of our mutilated Rocky Mountain, something that tells us we ought to deliberate and to act.

We have never been content to simply let the park be. Nor should we, for at this late date in its history, its well-being has become our responsibility, whether we will it or not. Is "natural regulation" working? Is "natural regulation" science, in the sense that it formulates testable hypotheses? The pride and glory of our science is its willingness to question authority.

I can sympathize with readers who will find *Rocky Times* somehow "ideological." But we all carry something of the barbarian in us, don't we? We all are reluctant to ask ourselves fundamental questions about history and ecology. To understand how Rocky Mountain got into such a mess, however, we must scrutinize the process of people thinking about nature. We must study the perceptions and values people have about the nonhuman world, no matter how painful and humbling this process might be.

Karl Hess has done his homework. He is our ally in this process, just as he is Rocky Mountain's ally. Since the late 1970s he has spent more productive time in the woods of northern Colorado than anyone else I know. His work with the Park Service and the Forest Service amply qualified him to write *Rocky Times,* a book that shows he belongs in the big leagues with forest ecologists like Robert Peet and the late Robert Alexander.

But Hess has gone a step further. He has moved from describing what is to describing what ought to be, from the realm of science to the realm of ethics, and from there to the realm of natural resource policy. Finally, Hess is true to his roots at Colorado State University, an institution traditionally oriented to problem solving and to action in the face of natural resource management problems. Hess gives those who care about the park exactly what Professor Limerick says we need—a balance sheet of gains and losses: gains that can be sustained and gains that prove temporary; injuries and losses where repair and recovery are imaginable; and injuries where repair and recovery are beyond imagination.

T.D.A. Cockerell of the University of Colorado was our first great ecologist. Toward the end of his long life, he wrote, "I think I have erred most in failing to act or speak where action was needed." Those were the words of a wise man.

Tom Wolf
Adjunct Professor
Southwest Studies Program
Colorado College

Preface

There are good reasons for me to write about Rocky Mountain National Park. First, there is the issue of an ailing environment—the glaring evidence of decades of damage to the park's land and life. That damage mounts daily, becoming more conspicuous and more shameful with each passing season. Second, there is the pressing matter of public policy—the urgent need to develop approaches and institutions to properly care for special places like Rocky Mountain. These reasons alone are sufficient to compel me to stand up and speak out for the nation's parks. But in the case of Rocky Mountain National Park, there is another, more compelling reason—a reason that is deeply personal.

When I moved to Colorado in 1977, I had only the vaguest notion of what the land and life of the high Rockies were like. I knew nothing of the ecology of aspen, the life history of lodgepole pine, the behavior of elk, or the environmental needs of beaver and willow. All I knew—and all that I felt was necessary to understand—was the immediate and powerful presence of an awesome and beautiful landscape. It seemed enough to climb 14,000-foot peaks and to physically and spiritually experience the wildness of the Colorado Rockies. Opportunity changed that. I earned my Ph.D. in the field of plant ecology, living and researching in the forests, meadows, and alpine heights of the Arapaho and Roosevelt national forests, which surround Rocky Mountain National Park.

My work was part of a U.S. Forest Service project to inventory the plant species and communities of the Colorado Front Range. I studied and identified the habitat types of the Arapaho and Roosevelt national forests—the mosaic of persisting plant communities that stretch from the foothills to the highest peaks.[1] I became familiar with the ecology of aspen, the life history of lodgepole pine, the behavior of elk, and the environmental needs of beaver and willow. I spent thousands of hours walking beneath the dense canopies of blue spruce, climbing steep slopes of Douglas-fir, hiking across vast subalpine and alpine meadows, and venturing into the depths of old-growth spruce-fir forests. Like a duckling just hatched from its shell, I was hopelessly enamored of and irreversibly bound to what I saw. The central Colorado Rockies became my surrogate family—a marvelous and unequaled cross section of nature that continues to enliven my spirit, excite my imagination, and tenaciously claim my allegiance.

My love and knowledge of the Colorado Front Range brought me to Rocky Mountain National Park in 1988. The park's science staff had asked me to inventory the grasslands, shrublands, wetlands, and forests of Rocky Mountain. Although the focus of my work had shifted toward natural resources policy analysis, I eagerly accepted the offer.[2] It was an opportunity to reacquaint myself with a land and a diversity of life that had been important to me during the halcyon days of living and working in one of the most spectacular settings on Earth.

When I began my Rocky Mountain inventory, I assumed it would be a straightforward job of environmental reporting—recording species, describing plant communities, and delineating physical environments. At the start of the project, David Stevens and Henry McCutchen of the park's science staff tried to impress on me that the park was facing serious biological problems and that my work was somehow related to them.[3] At the time, however, those problems seemed distant and abstract compared to the immediate joy of being back home again. I had no reason to believe that they would mar my return or disrupt my pleasant escape from the stressful, cerebral world of policy analysis. I was back in Eden, and nothing would disrupt the joy of being there. By the time I completed my work three years later, however, I knew that my initial reaction had been wrong.[4] The environmental problems plaguing the park were far greater than I had imagined, and the policy implications of those problems were alarming. With my contractual obligations to the science staff completed, I turned my attention to the unsettling reality that had greeted my jubilant homecoming. I was determined to tell the story of Rocky Mountain in its entirety and to seek ways to improve the park's ecological fortunes.

Long before turning my attention to the problems and policies of Rocky Mountain National Park, I had become familiar with the debate surrounding the management and condition of Yellowstone National Park. I had met Alston Chase on numerous occasions and had read and reread his book, *Playing God in Yellowstone,* nearly as often. By the summer of 1990, I knew that Yellowstone was not an anomaly, that what was happening to the environment there was also occurring in my personal Eden. But the more I familiarized myself with the problems of Rocky Mountain National Park, the more I became convinced that Chase's perspective on Yellowstone—his reasoning regarding what was happening there and why—contributed little to explaining the appalling damage being done to Rocky Mountain's valleys, meadows, and forests. Intellectually and emotionally, I was repelled by Chase's virulent attacks on environmentalism. For all the philosophical failings of deep ecology, those ascribed to it by Chase seemed excessive and, in some cases, unreasonable and implausible. Moreover, his unbridled distaste for park rangers and his uncritical embrace of science and scientists appeared too facile—too neat and tidy to explain convincingly why a park like Yellowstone had fallen from natural grace and why empowering experts would restore and protect it in the future. For these and other reasons, I knew the story of Rocky Mountain would lead me to different conclusions and recommendations.

The approach I have taken in telling Rocky Mountain's story is my own. I firmly believe that the men and women who oversee Rocky Mountain on a daily basis are decent, caring people. I am also convinced that decent and caring people are insufficient safeguards for our national parks. David Stevens and Henry McCutchen, with whom I worked so closely, and the many naturalists and park rangers who see to Rocky Mountain's everyday needs operate in an institutional and policy environment that makes caring difficult and action almost impossible. This is not to say that people are to be absolved of responsibility for what by law is their duty. Rather, it is to suggest that the ecology of human action is so complex that blame cannot be easily assigned without first understanding the incentives that encourage and shape that action. In the case of Rocky Mountain National Park, those incentives have been more negative than positive and more destructive than beneficial.

In the pages that follow, I present a strongly worded and well-documented indictment of gross mismanagement of Rocky Mountain National Park. My words should not be read as an attack on particular people or as a critique of any particular version of a philosophy of nature. I have immense respect for the men and women of Rocky Mountain National Park and the visions of nature and naturalness that dwell in their hearts. Indeed, the implementation of my proposal for rescuing Rocky Mountain from three-quarters of a century of benign neglect rests squarely on their shoulders. It seeks reform that will give them cause to care and room to act. For that reason, my indictment should be seen as a personal cry of anguish for a beloved country and as a general call for aid to a much-beleaguered landscape.

Karl Hess, Jr.
Las Cruces, New Mexico

Acknowledgments

Many people have contributed to this book in many special ways. Financial support for research was provided by the Foundation for Research on Economics and the Environment. John Baden, chairman of that organization, was the catalyst behind *Rocky Times*. He urged me to write about my findings long before I had a clear idea of what I would say. His loyalty and friendship have made this book and other projects possible. The debt I owe him can only be repaid by unwavering friendship and the most profound respect.

I would be remiss if I failed to acknowledge the contributions of Rocky Mountain National Park's staff in the making of *Rocky Times*. Among the scientists and naturalists who guided me in my journey through the park, I owe very special thanks to David Stevens, Henry McCutchen, and Richard Keigley. Although this book reflects my views and interpretations, not theirs, its factual content rests on the decades' worth of study and research performed by these three ecologists. And despite the disagreement and criticism expressed in *Rocky Times,* I admire all three for doing the best they could under very adverse conditions. I have the highest regard for their capabilities and the greatest respect for their judgment. I firmly believe that if they—and their fellow park scientists, naturalists, and rangers—had been given the freedom and responsibility to act, Rocky Mountain National Park would be much closer to living up to its reputation as a biosphere reserve.

Numerous other individuals have scrutinized my work and offered invaluable assistance. I am particularly grateful to those who took the time to review my manuscript. I thank Ed Marston, publisher of *High Country News,* for his review of the first draft of the manuscript; Fred Wagner, of Utah State University, for his careful scrutiny of my text and his editorial contributions; Will Moir, U.S. Forest Service, Rocky Mountain Forest and Range Experiment Station, for his incisive and constructive comments; and my good friend Tom Wolf for the countless conversations and consultations between us during the final preparation of the text. Tom provided a critical sounding board at the most crucial moments.

Acknowledgments

I also wish to recognize Marianne Keddington. This is the second book of mine that she has changed for the better with her editorial skill. She has an impressive talent for separating the chaff from the wheat. Further, I am indebted to Shannon Lenz-Wall for the artistic talents she brought to *Rocky Times*. Her drawings grace the pages of this book and will always remind me of that splendid place called Rocky Mountain National Park. In addition, I am grateful to William Bradford for taking interest in my work and pushing for its initial publication in essay form.

Finally, I owe more than words can say to my ecology mentors, professors emeritus Edward Mogren and Clinton Wasser (both of the College of Natural Resources, Colorado State University). These two educators and ecologists guided me through four years of doctoral research at Colorado State University and provided their time and help during my three years of research at Rocky Mountain National Park. Their guidance and assistance, first as professors and later as colleagues and friends, served me well as I explored the valleys and mountains of the park and questioned three-quarters of a century of National Park Service management. Although the ecological interpretations and policy formulations offered in *Rocky Times* are uniquely mine, I cannot imagine having written one word of this book without having had the honor of knowing these two gentlemen.

K.H.

Rocky Times in Rocky Mountain National Park

CHAPTER 1

Introduction

MOUNTAIN MAJESTY

Capt. John R. Bell was the official journalist for the Long Expedition. His job was to record the expedition's trek west along the Platte River to the base of the Rocky Mountains. On Friday, June 30, 1820, he and his fellow explorers sighted a subtle change on the western horizon. What they spotted lay over a hundred miles away, barely perceptible above the seemingly endless expanse of rolling prairie. "We discovered," Bell wrote, "a blue strip, close in with the horizon to the west—which was by some pronounced to be no more than a cloud . . . [but] which to our great satisfaction and heart felt joy, was declared by the commanding officer to be the range of the Rocky Mountains . . . [and] a high Peake was plainly to be distinguished towering above all others as far as the sight extended."[1]

The summit they saw in the distance was Longs Peak—the namesake of Maj. Stephen Harriman Long, commander of the congressionally mandated scientific expedition. The sighting elated Bell. "The whole range had a beautiful and sublime appearance to us," Bell recorded, "after having been so long confined to the dull and uninteresting monotony of prairie country."[2] Months of traveling had brought them to the mountain majesty of the Front Range of the Colorado Rockies and to the enclave of towering peaks that would one day become Rocky Mountain National Park.

Today Longs Peak, standing sentinel over the northeastern Colorado plains, is the enduring symbol of the beauty and majesty of Rocky Mountain National Park. Its 14,225-foot-high summit of bare, angular granite is framed by flower-bedecked alpine peneplains, abrupt subalpine slopes cloaked in spruce-fir and lodgepole pine, and stark montane hills and valleys dotted with ponderosa pine and grassy openings. The scene is captivating, whether it is being viewed for the first or the hundredth time. The harmony of rock, tundra, and strikingly uniform forests presents a portrait of near-pristine

"A blue strip, close in with the horizon to the west . . . [and] a high Peake." Drawing by Shannon Lenz-Wall.

nature and untrammeled wilderness. Few other landscapes can compare with this small slice of the Front Range of the Rocky Mountains, just fifty miles north of Denver.

The uniqueness of Rocky Mountain National Park stretches back to an age when elk, wolves, and grizzly bears shared the mountain enclave with Native Americans. As long ago as 3850 B.C., native peoples camped and hunted in the valleys, mountains, and tundra of what is now the park.[3] Plains Indians used the "Two Guide," Longs Peak and its neighbor, Mount Meeker, as critical landmarks in their migrations.[4] The Ute and Arapaho tribes—and sometimes the Cheyenne and Shoshone—traveled the Continental Divide along trails that still crisscross the park. Except for occasional trappers and explorers, however, the land that was to become the park remained a mystery to non-Indian settlers until the outbreak of the American Civil War. Spanish and French mountain men had known of the area since the mid-eighteenth century, having named the twin peaks of Longs and Meeker "les Deux Oreilles"—the Two Ears. The scientific expeditions led by Lt. Zebulon Pike in 1806 and by Maj. Stephen Long in 1820 had noted the towering summit of Longs Peak and the sublime beauty of the rising Front Range against the backdrop of rolling prairie. But it was not until 1859 and the arrival of Joel Estes that permanent settlement of the area by Europeans began in earnest.

What attracted settlers like Estes to the mountain enclave was the expansive grassland, or more correctly *park,* that lay at the foot of the high

Rockies—a broad and relatively flat opening in the montane forest, encircled by a horseshoe pattern of snow-capped peaks. Extensive meadows and gently sloping hills extended the park for miles in all directions, its continuity disrupted only by clear mountain streams and the granite boundaries of 12,000- to 14,000-foot-high mountains. Abundant grass and a climate moderated by frequent chinook winds made the park—named Estes Park after its first permanent resident—prime cattle country. Settlers drawn to it filled the mountain valley. They carved homes out of the wilderness, built ranches, hunted the park's abundant wildlife, and, in the process, shattered the rule of Eden over the area. "In 1875," wrote Abner Sprague, an early homesteader in Estes Park, "the elk came down from the mountains by the thousands and were met by hunters with repeating rifles and four-horse teams. In 1876, few elk came down and, by 1877, very few were seen east of the Continental Divide.'[5]

Abner Sprague saw and hunted his last elk the following year. By then, cattle were king both in Estes Park and in the valleys and meadows of the encircling high country. By 1900 Milton Estes, an Estes Park rancher and son of the first settler, was lamenting the excessive grazing that was denuding the park and transforming its once abundant grasslands into weedy patches.[6] At the same time, naturalists watched with resignation as grizzly bears and wolves made their final stands.[7]

Unlike other mountain communities along the Colorado Front Range, Estes Park and the surrounding summits were able to escape the worst environmental abuses that came with mining and excessive logging. Prospectors came and went, and even one substantial mining town—Lulu City—was established west of the Continental Divide and thrived from 1880 to 1884; but valuable minerals were never abundant in the granite, gneiss, and schist bedrock of the area. Because mining stopped early in the park's history, extensive timber markets did not develop, large sawmills were never established, and logging was largely restricted to home building and fence construction.[8]

More importantly, Estes Park—and the city of Estes Park, incorporated in 1917—quickly earned a reputation among tourists for fine lodges, unsurpassed scenery, and excellent trout fishing. By the turn of the century, traditional livestock operations were being converted to part-time dude ranches. Natural and economic forces had become emphatically clear: this mountain enclave's highest value lay in its scenery and wildlife, not in its minerals, timber, and harvestable grass. By virtue of its beauty and majesty, the area was spared the flurry of commercial activity that gouged and pocked the landscapes of much of the Colorado Front Range.

Rocky Mountain's reputation for beauty and majesty is as old as its first ranching settlements. Isabella Bird, a visitor to Estes Park in 1873, wrote, "Never, anywhere, have I seen anything equal to the view into Estes Park."[9] Albert Bierstadt, the celebrated landscape artist, painted his famous portrait of Longs Peak in 1874, and the painting hung in the Capitol rotunda in Washington for years. Ferdinand V. Hayden, who led three expeditions to Yellowstone National Park during the 1870s, visited the area that was to become Rocky Mountain in 1875 and recorded his strong reaction: "Within the district treated [the Front Range of the Rocky Mountains] we will scarcely be able to find a region so favorably distinguished. Not only has nature amply supplied this valley with features of rare beauty and surroundings of admirable grandeur, but it has thus distributed them that the eye of an artist may rest with perfect satisfaction on the complete picture presented."[10]

Among the visitors captivated by the mountain landscape was a young man from Kansas, Enos A. Mills, who arrived in Estes Park in 1884 at the age of fourteen. He took what jobs he could find, mostly herding and caring for livestock. But days and weeks living and working in the outdoors shifted his attention from the obligations of ranching to the preservation of nature. Mills's life changed from that of a cowboy and guide to a full-time protector and preserver of the meadows and peaks. Years later, Mills fondly recalled the beauty that had surrounded him when he worked as a wrangler. "The striking characteristics of the Rocky Mountains are here seen at their best. The high rugged peaks are set with lovely spaces, primeval forests, scattered groves, and eternal snowfields; the mountain slopes and intervening valleys are splendidly adorned with spruces, great pines, and restless aspens. It is a monumental garden spot of loveliness and grandeur."[11]

The first step to protect the area was taken in 1905, when President Theodore Roosevelt withdrew the lands that were to become Rocky Mountain from the public domain and merged them with the Medicine Bow Forest Reserve in southern Wyoming. Making Estes Park and the mountains above it part of a forest reserve, however, was not enough for Enos Mills. "Though a Forest Reserve, like a farm, has beauty," Mills concluded, "it is not established for its beauty but for practical use."[12] With that thought in mind, in 1909 Mills embarked on a one-man crusade to have the area designated a national park. After delivering forty-two lectures, writing sixty-four newspaper articles and over two thousand letters, and overcoming U.S. Forest Service opposition, Mills achieved his goal.[13] On September 4, 1915, Rocky Mountain National Park was dedicated "for the preservation of the natural conditions and scenic beauties thereof."[14]

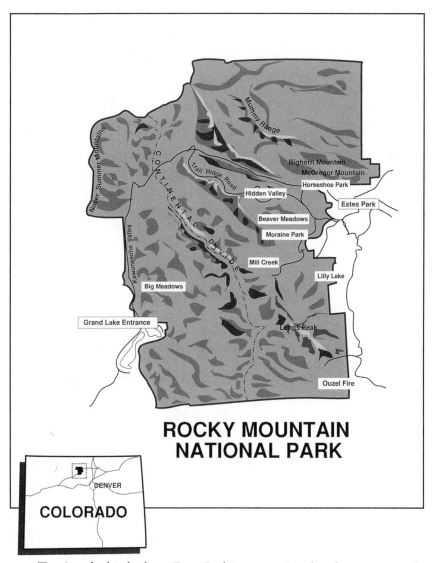

Mummy Range

Never Summer Mountains

C O N T I N E N T A L

Trail Ridge Road

Bighorn Mountain
McGregor Mountain
Horseshoe Park

Hidden Valley

Estes Park

Beaver Meadows

Moraine Park

Kawuneeche Valley

D I V I D E

Mill Creek

Lilly Lake

Big Meadows

Grand Lake Entrance

Longs Peak

Ouzel Fire

**ROCKY MOUNTAIN
NATIONAL PARK**

DENVER

COLORADO

Turning the lands above Estes Park into a national park meant consoli-
dating landownership and phasing out livestock grazing and other commercial activities. By 1962 the last enclave of grazing on the east side of the park
(with the minor exception of Black Canyon) was eliminated when portions
of Moraine Park were acquired. Grazing on the west side of the park ended
with the purchase of the Never Summer Ranch from The Nature Conservancy

in 1975. In addition, the final vestiges of commercial activity—including a small golf course at the lower end of Moraine Park—were bulldozed and the cleared landscapes rehabilitated. Rocky Mountain National Park—a thin "blue strip" to John Bell and his comrades in 1820—was now complete.

Today Rocky Mountain is one of fifty parks and 69 million acres managed by the National Park Service. Encompassing 265,000 acres, it is tiny compared to the 8.3-million-acre Wrangell–St. Elias National Park in Alaska—or, for that matter, the seven other Alaskan parks, whose total area encompasses over 22 million acres. Yet in the lower forty-eight states, Rocky Mountain is substantial. Yellowstone, Olympic, Grand Canyon, Big Bend, Everglades, and Glacier national parks may be larger, but in terms of unparalleled scenery packed into such a compact space, there is no competition.

The park takes up a twenty-five-mile stretch of the Continental Divide. It begins in the north in the alpine tundra of the Mummy Range and extends south beyond Longs Peak to the northern terminus of the Indian Peaks Wilderness Area. East of the Continental Divide, the park is bounded by the city of Estes Park and State Highway 7. West of the divide, it encompasses the lengthy Kawuneeche Valley and the soaring summits of the Never Summer Mountains. Although only 3,000 acres of the park are currently designated as wilderness, and therefore are protected by federal law as a primitive area free of "the imprint of man's work,"[15] an additional 235,000 acres have been proposed for inclusion in the national wilderness system.

Apart from the large areas of Rocky Mountain that are covered in barren rock and talus slopes, almost half the remainder of the park that does support plant life is clothed in open grasslands and wet marshes. The majority of that vegetation lies above timberline in the alpine world of persisting glaciers and late-melting snowfields. Below, in Estes Park, dry grasslands intermingle with sagebrush, wet meadows, and stands of willow. Between the two grassland biomes are the montane and subalpine regions of ponderosa pine woodlands, Douglas-fir-forested montane slopes, aspen groves, and lodgepole pine and spruce-fir forests. High mountain meadows and subalpine lakes round out the park's diverse landscape.

Many features add to the environmental richness of the nation's tenth-oldest national park. The headwaters of the Colorado River flow from the upper reaches of the Kawuneeche Valley. Over 133 peaks soar above 10,000 feet. Scores of lakes and dozens of streams dot and dissect the mountain majesty of Rocky Mountain. Ancient forests, near-pristine alpine tundra, and multitudes of animal and plant species provide a research haven for botanists, wildlife biologists, and research ecologists. Best of all, the biological and ecological wonders of Rocky Mountain are packed into a compact 414-

square-mile package that can be accessed with relative ease from almost any corner. Ranging from 7,800 feet to 14,225 feet in elevation, the park encompasses all the vegetation zones and major vegetation types of the central Rocky Mountains.[16]

It is not surprising, then, that Rocky Mountain—twenty-third in size among its sister parks—is the sixth most heavily visited park in the nation. With an annual visitation in 1991 of 2,903,811, Rocky Mountain had just 55,000 fewer visitors than its more celebrated sibling, Yellowstone (2,958,000 visitors in 1991).[17] Such a level of visitation is especially notable given the relative distance of Rocky Mountain from the densely populated urban centers that serve the more popular Great Smoky Mountains, Acadia, Grand Canyon, and Yosemite national parks.

Rocky Mountain's importance, however, clearly transcends the visitor statistics. The park's beauty and majesty cannot be measured or understood in terms of the momentary rapture that envelops the millions of tourists that drive its roads and hike its trails. Biologically and ecologically, the park is unequaled. Its diverse landscapes, concentrated in one small enclave of the Colorado Front Range, are a vivid reminder of all the features that mark the Rocky Mountains as special and unique. As testimony to these qualities and in recognition of the park's place in the global biome, the United Nations' UNESCO Man and the Biosphere Program designated Rocky Mountain a biosphere reserve in 1976. The plaque commemorating that designation, which is housed in the park's main headquarters, speaks to the ideals and expectations that Rocky Mountain stands for and sets high standards for the park's purpose, function, and preservation: "Rocky Mountain National Park is recognized as part of the international network of biosphere reserves. This network of protected samples of the world's major ecosystem types is devoted to conservation of nature and scientific research in the service of man. *It provides a standard against which the effect of man's impact on his environment can be measured.*"[18]

The designation of Rocky Mountain as a biosphere reserve declares to local residents, visitors, and the global community that the mountain enclave is special—that its peaks and valleys are a deserving symbol and a proper preserve for the incomparable Rocky Mountain chain. But as fitting as it may be, the designation lacks the force of law; it carries no weight in the system of American jurisprudence. The designation of biosphere reserve merely sets a desirable direction for policy and management, a suggested course of action to bolster and enhance the legislated mandate for preserving and protecting Rocky Mountain's ecology and environment.

Not surprisingly, the designation says nothing about the results of being preserved and protected as a biosphere reserve. It offers no hint of how the park is faring or whether the plants and animals that dwell within its boundaries are thriving. Most of all, the designation is conspicuously silent on whether the ideals embodied by the international network of biosphere reserves have been adopted and upheld by the park's custodians. To measure results—to know if the mountain enclave is truly a *standard against which the effect of man's impact on his environment can be measured*—we must focus on the land and life of Rocky Mountain National Park. We must take the pulse of its meadows and forests and note the vital signs of its beavers and bears.

DISQUIETING SIGNS

Rocky Mountain National Park is almost picture perfect. Granite peaks tower above alpine meadows; snowfields temper the heat of the summer sun; uniformly forested slopes rise steeply from grassy valley bottoms; shimmering streams trail from turquoise lakes; yellowing aspens quake in the breeze of a late summer afternoon; and bull elk lift their antlered heads and bugle their mating call, breaking the stillness of a fall morning. In the background, framing peaks and valleys and quaking aspens, is the azure blue of the Rocky Mountain sky. These are the scenes that captivate park visitors and lure them back again and again.

Two minor defects, both of which are common knowledge, just barely mar this vision of Rocky Mountain. Years ago, just after Trail Ridge Road (the highest continuous paved roadway in the world) was opened to alpine travel in 1933 and when visitors were still free to walk on the fragile tundra, damage was done. Soils were compacted and eroded along popular roadsides and trails, and the few plant species that could survive in the harsh alpine environment were trampled and destroyed. In the 1950s and 1960s, the Park Service began to restore the damaged areas. Tourist access was restricted and controlled, and heavily impacted sites were treated and protected. Today, even though disturbed areas of the tundra have been vastly improved, the signs of abuse endure, testimony to the fragility and slow-paced resilience of high-altitude alpine biomes.[19]

The other noticeable defect of Rocky Mountain National Park is the increasing number of visitors. Long lines of traffic and congestion on the most popular trails diminish the serenity and wildness of Rocky Mountain. Popular spots like Bear Lake have become so crowded that parking lots are often filled by midmorning. To relieve traffic and parking congestion, shuttle buses run to and from the lake. Elsewhere in the park there are bumper-to-bumper traffic jams, and unmanageable numbers of onlookers frequently clog the scenic overlooks. Early mornings and late evenings offer a relative reprieve to visitors seeking to escape long lines of people and cars.

In the larger perspective, however, an acre or two of trampled tundra and periodic overflows of visitors are trifling imperfections. They in no way compromise Rocky Mountain's designation and role as a biosphere reserve. The fact is that no people walk on most of Rocky Mountain's alpine tundra. Visitors rarely venture to the hidden valleys and the high alpine lakes, apparently content to see the park from a few well-manicured trails. Most of the park's valleys and summits are shielded from the long lines of cars and mounting numbers of tourists that the summer brings. "Sublime" and "undisturbed" are still the best words to describe the park's inaccessible places.

A near-picture-perfect Rocky Mountain National Park would seem to be a tribute to the ideals of the international system of biosphere reserves. Certainly, there is no doubt about the splendor of the park's environment, the unique ecological values tucked away in its remote corners, and the overwhelming aesthetics that greet millions of visitors each year. The designation of biosphere reserve announces that Rocky Mountain is special and that by all visual evidence the park is living up to its reputation as a unique and protected pocket of pristine nature. But to conclude from such impressionistic evidence that the park is being protected, that its managers are somehow uniquely devoted to its conservation, or that it really does provide "a standard against which the effect of man's impact on his environment can be measured" would be a tragic error. Beneath the veneer of granite peaks, alpine tundra, and uniform forests is a far less attractive picture—a picture of anything but environmental health and ecological soundness. The other side of Rocky Mountain—the disquieting face of a landscape in crisis—is not visible in the sweeping panorama that encompasses towering peaks, alpine expanses, subalpine forests, lush green valleys, montane woodlands, and open grasslands. It is not to be found in the fragile alpine tundra where park administrators and scientists have focused their time, dollars, and research to protect and preserve what seemed most threatened, and what millions of visitors longed most to see. But this is not surprising.

The region above timberline was never as fragile as administrators and scientists assumed. Conversely, the forests and grasslands below tree line were never as sturdy and safe as conventional wisdom dictated. Among the trees and meadows, obscured by the deceptive harmony of uniform forests and picturesque grassy openings, ecological decline and environmental decay are most evident and most threatening. By walking into the park's forests, exploring the meadows, and looking carefully at the thin mantle of soil that supports it all, we can see beyond the images to the illness striking at Rocky Mountain National Park.

One of America's premier parks is experiencing rocky times, relentlessly moving toward an ecological Armageddon. The assumptions and practices of protection and preservation are meeting the reality of environmental decadence and decline. The presumed efficacy of federal ownership of America's finest landscapes is no longer the simple matter of faith in experts and blind belief in a long-cherished American institution. The evidence of three-quarters of a century of mismanagement by the National Park Service—mismanagement that has abandoned Rocky Mountain to the vagaries of public policy—is too compelling. Faith and belief are simply overwhelmed by the dissonance between what should be and what is.

Symptomatic of the illness and the approaching Armageddon is the park's meadow showcase, Moraine Park, at the modest elevation of 8,000 feet. To the untutored eye, all appears well. A lively stream bisects a large, grassy clearing, bordered on the north and south by glacial moraines forested in ponderosa pine, lodgepole pine, and Douglas-fir. Closer inspection, though, reveals disquieting signs. Across the northern moraine, obtrusive signs of elk clutter the lodgepole pine forest floor. The thick mat of pine needles is covered with multiple layers of manure. The dense concentrations of scat evoke the images and smells of a stockyard. In the clearing, past a ponderosa pine woodland, an increasing density of younger ponderosas appears to be choking out a rich understory of shrubs, forbs, and grasses that feed many of the park's deer and elk.

Beyond the thickening stand of ponderosa pine, dead and dying willows dotting the abnormally dry mountain meadow catch the eye. At certain spots, the stream cuts unusually deep into the dry meadow soil, exposing raw vertical banks three to four feet high. The flats are full of weeds, and obnoxious Canadian thistles are abundant, as is the presence of animal scat. Plant species normally abundant in mountain meadows, such as tufted hairgrass, have almost disappeared. Replacing them are invading species, like needle-and-thread grass, that thrive on disturbance at higher elevations and favor the desiccating environment of the park. Ahead, up the moraine bordering the park's southern edge, the signs are even more disturbing. The steep slope of the moraine is covered by dead and dying trees, the remnant of a once-vigorous stand of Douglas-fir. Western spruce budworm disease has ravaged nearly 90 percent of the forest stand. Within its skeletal remains, a forest floor that once

One of the worst examples of active soil erosion in Rocky Mountain National Park is found in upper Beaver Meadows. Top photograph shows a deepening (over 2 meters) and widening stream cut. The damage is largely attributable to the cumulative effects of elk destruction of streambank willow communities, loss of beaver dams, and grazing-induced soil compaction. Bottom photograph shows remnant of a formerly dense riparian stand adjacent to the cut. Willows have been eliminated by elk, leaving only unpalatable alder. Even worse, the water table of the surrounding meadow is falling as the stream cut deepens. What was once a wet meadow of high plant density and diversity is becoming a desiccated and denuded landscape. Photographs by author (June 1993).

Top photograph shows small herd of bull elk grazing in Moraine Park. Note the near absence of willows and riparian vegetation along the meandering stream in the background. Bottom photograph depicts one of several elk-trampled springs that dot the landscape of Moraine Park. Note the darker patches of vegetation in the background. These patches are made up almost exclusively of Baltic rush and are expanding in size due to heavy elk grazing. The ecological cost of their expansion is loss of meadow diversity. Photographs by author (June 1993).

was luxuriantly vegetated now consists of trampled soil covered with a smelly mantle of elk manure—a scene already witnessed on the northernmost moraine.

Trails made by elk cut deeply into the moraine and funnel erosive waters toward the meadow below. The few Douglas-fir trees still alive are scarred and sometimes almost fully girdled—the effect of too many elk horns rubbing against too few trees. Aspen intermixed with ponderosa pine on the northern moraine are visible through the tangle of dead and dying branches. Also scarred by elk and infected by a fatal fungus, they are sharing the fate of the disappearing Douglas-fir.[20]

Sadly, this picture of Moraine Park is not an anomaly. Similar symptoms of environmental decay plague Rocky Mountain National Park in almost every valley bottom and on almost every mountain slope. Contrary to the impressions of majesty and serenity that color one's first glance of the park, close-up reality paints an altogether different portrait. The park is not "a standard against which the effect of man's impact on his environment can be measured." It is, instead, a testament to how damaging that impact can be, particularly in a setting of such awesome beauty and high ecological potential.

Surprisingly, little has been said or written about the serious ecological problems facing Rocky Mountain. Apart from expressions of misgivings about too many visitors and persistent concerns regarding old tundra scars, a curtain of administrative silence shrouds the valleys and peaks. Of the almost four hundred naturalist and scientific works on the park—almost all of them paid for by federal dollars—only a small number allude to Rocky Mountain's problems and only a handful (mostly published before 1956) address the pressing issue of the park's environmental health.[21] The rest focus on more theoretical and esoteric aspects of the park's land and life. Indeed, administrators and researchers have pursued their studies seemingly oblivious to resource conditions and long-range ecological trends.

The poverty of the official record does not mean that those who have studied and written about the park are unaware of the threats to its ecological integrity. Staff biologists at Rocky Mountain and professors and researchers at Colorado State University and the University of Colorado are candid in their personal judgments: Rocky Mountain National Park is in grave danger.[22] All of them are aware of places like Moraine Park. All of them understand the nature of the problem. But none of them has chosen to speak or write in public about what is happening to the park. The shroud of silence preserves and protects management policies whose primary legacy is the mounting loss of plant community diversity and the disruption of wildlife.

And silence deepens the crisis and makes the reality of ecological disruption and environmental destruction all the more unacceptable and inexcusable. In a most fundamental sense, Rocky Mountain's crisis is one of mismanagement and bureaucratic ineptitude—a crisis connected with a laissez-faire approach to elk population control and a long history of fire suppression. In the final analysis, the crisis is caused by the failure of public policy and the distortions imposed on land management by political and bureaucratic considerations.

CHAPTER 2

Beasts of Plunder

ELK ON THE RAMPAGE

Two events of significance to Rocky Mountain happened in 1915. First, Rocky Mountain National Park was established. Second, elk once again grazed the valleys and meadows of Estes Park. The elk had been hunted to extinction by 1900, but in 1913 and 1914, 49 elk from the Yellowstone herd were transplanted to Estes Park.[1] Although mortality was initially high, the herd began producing calves and quickly stabilized at 30 head by 1915. Three years later, the head count was up to 60; by 1921 it had soared to an estimated 120. The brief rule of the cattle kingdom in Rocky Mountain had come to an end.

For Enos Mills and his supporters, the attainment of national park status was momentous. Such status, they believed, would achieve the desired goals of preservation and protection. The beauty and diversity that made Rocky Mountain such a special place would be held in trust for future generations by people dedicated to the park's welfare and perpetuation. Reintroducing elk would undoubtedly contribute to the park's restoration, but making Rocky Mountain a national park was by far the most important step. In 1915 Mills and his supporters could not have imagined that a small herd of elk might one day undo all the good they hoped would come from Rocky Mountain's new privileged status.

The transplanted Yellowstone elk quickly became the focus of local pride and protection. By 1929, when the animals were staging a remarkable recovery throughout Colorado and the herd in the park had exceeded 300 head, Estes Park residents were fighting a state proposal to create a hunting season for elk. On July 19, 1929, the Estes Park *Trail* reported that "the proposal of some in the state for an open season on elk naturally does not meet with the most hearty approval of Estes Park people who spent so much time and money to re-introduce elk into the state." Two years later, the *Trail* reported more hostility among local residents to elk hunting—even though the official herd count was now up to 430. Elk, the paper opined, were to be observed and enjoyed, not hunted and slaughtered: "Valley folk and tourists from at least ten states outside Colorado were park visitors over the week-end. . . . High Drive was a busy thoroughfare all day as villagers and visitors made the round trip to view the herd of elk in Horseshoe Park and to see the numerous deer that are to be found on the famous circle trip."[2]

As the Estes Park *Trail* echoed the protective sentiments of local residents, National Park Service staff were beginning to voice concerns over the mushrooming herd. John McLaughlin, chief ranger for Rocky Mountain National Park, sounded a warning in his 1931 wildlife report:

> Last winter, for the first time, the elk began tearing bark off aspen trees. This is the first season this has really been noticeable, although many of the aspen groves have really suffered heavily—in just one season. Examination shows that the elk have barked the aspens before, but never to the extent that they did last winter. The range generally is in very poor condition. It is overgrazed to the extent that in many places the original ground cover has been destroyed, and the mineral soil has been exposed to erosion, or is rapidly being occupied by undesirable plants and weeds.[3]

Two years after McLaughlin's report, a special task force on wildlife problems in national parks concluded that "there are now believed to be approximately 350 [elk] in the area, and Rocky Mountain National Park is already faced with an elk problem."[4]

The emerging problem was largely one of limited winter range in the park. During summer the expanding elk herd could find abundant forage on alpine grasslands and in subalpine meadows. In winter months, however, when heavy snows forced them down from the high country, the elk were largely dependent on Rocky Mountain's low-elevation valleys for food, where the forage available was only a fraction of that in the more spacious mountains and tundra above. In other words, the park's high summer range had more than enough food to support 350 head of elk and enough space to ensure minimal damage to vegetation from grazing. The winter range was another matter. By most accounts, the elk herd in 1933 had met or exceeded the carrying capacity of the park's low-elevation valleys. There was simply not enough food to support the elk herd without noticeable and, in some cases, damaging effects on vegetation.

The immediate response of the Park Service was to acquire additional winter range for the elk herd. Over 12,000 acres of the winter range that had been stocked for and grazed by cattle were purchased and set aside in the early

1930s for the exclusive use of Rocky Mountain's elk. Except for portions of Moraine Park (acquired in 1962), the park's winter range was now as complete and as large as it could be, given the geography of Estes Park and the private lands that bordered the park on the east.

A report issued in 1931 by park biologist Joseph Dixon, however, questioned the long-term benefit of securing additional winter range:

> A careful study of the range plants and brush showed clearly that the present winter range within the park is entirely inadequate for the elk and deer now on hand and further investigation showed that even with the acquisition of the proposed additions, the carrying capacity of the winter range would not be sufficient for more than the present supply of game now in the park. The other alternative to securing more winter range would be to reduce the present stock of game in the park and this to the writer seems inadvisable.[5]

Dixon's warning on the limits of the winter range was filed and forgotten, and by 1935 elk numbers on Rocky Mountain's winter range had swollen to an estimated 550. The superintendent of Rocky Mountain reported in 1938 that "elk are increasing steadily though not rapidly throughout the Park. The herd is in good condition and there is no immediate forage problem."[6] The next year, the elk population reached an all-time estimated high of 1,210 head.[7]

The superintendent's optimistic words simply did not agree with what Dixon was observing on the ground. Elk numbers had not just expanded; they had overwhelmed the park's winter range. "Elk have [now] reached and passed the carrying capacity of the winter range," wrote Dixon in the late summer of 1939, "and are destroying it through over browsing." Further, he observed, "it would be possible to let the elk continue to breed up until decimated by starvation during some severe snowy winter. This would be neither humane nor wise management, and I think a slight annual pruning is preferable. I believe all agree that we should have all the elk in Rocky Mountain National Park that the limited range will support. The problem is what to do with the surplus."[8]

A year later, Fred Packard, a wildlife biologist with the Civilian Conservation Corps, reported to the Park Service, "My personal opinion is that the [elk] herds should be reduced by 50%." He later wrote, "A review of previous reports on the range problem in Rocky Mountain National Park demonstrates a serious deterioration of the forage plants on the lands of the district where deer and elk concentrate in winter." Unless action was taken, he warned, Rocky Mountain's winter-range elk herd might continue to grow at the remarkable annual rate of 45 percent.[9]

Packard and Dixon were at odds with the pro-elk stance of the majority of Rocky Mountain's staff and of the residents of Estes Park. What most people wanted—and what the park's superintendent was more than happy to provide—was more elk. To counter what he believed to be a sentimental and environmentally destructive attachment to elk, wildlife biologist Harold Ratcliff published a series of articles explaining the elk problem developing at Rocky Mountain National Park. His first article, published for the sixth North American Wildlife Conference in 1941, summarized the damage done to the winter range by excessive numbers of elk. Mill Creek, he wrote, "as a whole is very heavily utilized . . . [and] an ever-increasing number of weeds and less palatable species is coming into the composition of the range forage." At Moraine Park, he continued, "the trees have a very definite browse line . . . [and] trunks of aspen are scarred by the grazing of elk and there is very little reproduction." Beaver Meadows, "one of the most important parts of the entire winter range," was in even worse condition due to heavy elk grazing. "As much as 90 percent of the annual growth of the willows along the stream," Ratcliff observed, "is eaten with resulting increase in mortality." Reporting that the Rocky Mountain elk herd had increased from 30 head in 1915 to an estimated 1,100 head in 1940, Ratcliff warned that

> the increase of the elk herds that do not migrate beyond the eastern boundary of the park has reached a dangerous crisis. This overpopulation is utilizing available forage to an extent that can no longer be sustained without irreparable damage to the range.
>
> Reduction of the numbers of elk and deer must inevitably result. It will be either artificial, for which there is no present authorization, or natural, through starvation and disease. The gravest need at present is for legal authority to dispose of surplus animals.[10]

Authority to do something about Rocky Mountain's mounting elk problem came three years later. Getting to that point, however, required the combined efforts of Dixon, Packard, and Ratcliff. They published articles in the popular press to sway public opinion, delivered papers at scientific meetings to persuade wildlife biologists, and wrote report after report to the park superintendent on the deteriorating condition of Rocky Mountain. In addition, the proper carrying capacity of the park's winter range was debated among park staff, with estimates ranging from 400 to 1,400 head.[11] Finally, in late 1943 David Condon, the park naturalist for Rocky Mountain, concluded that 400 head of elk was the appropriate carrying capacity of the park's winter range and recommended that "the elk . . . in Rocky Mountain National Park be reduced to and maintained at the optimum numbers for the available range."[12]

On January 11, 1944, Secretary of the Interior Harold L. Ickes granted authority to Rocky Mountain National Park to reduce its resident elk herd. Eleven months later the program of elk control began with the shooting of over 300 animals by park rangers. From an estimated peak population of 1,525 in 1942, herd numbers on the winter range were more than halved in subsequent years, bringing them considerably closer to the estimated carrying capacity of 400.[13] Except for an increase in 1949, the estimated population of elk on Rocky Mountain's winter range remained well below 1,000 through 1967—a population level maintained by shooting through 1961 and thereafter by trapping and relocation. The park reported an average estimated elk population of 587 during this period, with a high of 1,072 in 1949 and a low of 350 in 1962.[14]

Vegetation conditions on Rocky Mountain's winter range improved dramatically during the years following 1944. Regional park biologist James E. Cole reported in 1953 that Rocky Mountain's elk control program was meeting its objectives. "The elk control operation is producing beneficial results," he observed, "and substantial range restoration is occurring."[15] A year later, a special report issued by Rocky Mountain concluded that "to date, marked restoration of ground cover has retarded, and in places, halted erosion . . . [and] native bunch grasses are coming back and may, if not again subjected to abuse, choke out the cheat grass."[16] Finally, in 1955 Robert Buttery completed a comprehensive study of range conditions resulting from winter concentrations of elk in the park. He concluded that "excess numbers of elk seriously damage[d] the range, particularly during the 1930s." More to the point, Buttery noted that the elk control program had resulted in improved ecological conditions for the park's major winter-range plant communities. "Findings of the study," he wrote, "showed . . . a slightly upward trend . . . on most areas."[17] Not surprisingly, Buttery recommended that the park's elk control program be continued indefinitely.

AN EXPERIMENT IN NATURAL REGULATION

Support for Rocky Mountain's elk control program was not unanimous. Shortly after its inception, Russell Grater, the park naturalist who had replaced David Condon, took issue with his predecessor's conclusions. He was certain that "from the standpoint of elk, it is now apparent that no serious problem has existed in the past at Rocky Mountain nor had one reached a really serious point at the time of the reduction program. This conclusion is reached only after noting the overall excellent condition of the herd and checking the available food supply."[18]

Although Grater's conclusion was at odds with the many scientific accounts of serious resource degradation in the park, his ideas reflected a strong sentiment within the National Park Service that the elk problem would have eventually taken care of itself if humans had not intervened. Hillory Tolson, assistant director of the National Park Service in 1946, added a caveat to Grater's message by making it clear that "this office has a strong dislike for 'reduction programs' either inside or adjacent to the National Parks."[19]

Grater's sentiments—reinforced by National Park Service policies, increasing pressure from hunting groups, and the persisting distaste among Estes Park residents for the reduction program—encouraged park administrators to rethink Rocky Mountain's approach to the elk problem. For years, the idea of using hunting *outside* the park as a means to control the elk population *within* the park had been discussed, but no concerted action had been taken to test the idea's soundness. All of that changed in 1962, when Rocky Mountain National Park signed a "memorandum of understanding" (MOU) with the U.S. Forest Service and the Colorado Division of Wildlife to cooperatively study management of the park's resident elk herd. The shooting of elk by park rangers ended with the signing of the MOU, and a special hunt was held in January 1963 along the park's eastern boundary, the entry point to Rocky Mountain's vital winter range. Although park rangers continued to trap and relocate small numbers of elk until as late as 1968, the three agencies agreed in principle that hunter harvest outside Rocky Mountain was the preferred means of controlling elk within the park's protected winter range.[20]

More data were needed, however, before Rocky Mountain and its cooperating agencies could turn hunting into an effective tool for elk control. They needed to know when the animals migrated from the high country to the winter range, and they needed information on the patterns of elk movement within the winter range. They also needed a solid estimate of the size of the winter range and its effective carrying capacity. Until this information was available, the location, timing, and size of hunts could not be definitely set and the control of elk on the winter range could not be optimized.

The first report of the cooperative tri-agency elk project was released in April 1964. In addition to outlining the history of the elk problem and the methods to be used in studying elk behavior and elk winter range, the report discussed how there came to be too many elk in Rocky Mountain National Park. "Accelerated human habitation and development in the Estes Park region," the authors concluded, "were largely responsible for the blocking of historic migration routes and winter ranges in the foothills and eastward." Cut off from winter range elsewhere along the eastern Front Range and blocked from migrating out of the park, Rocky Mountain's elk had no choice but to overgraze the park's meadows, willows, and aspen. Because of this, the report continued, "these studies are designed to develop a satisfactory solution to the surplus elk problem in the Park . . . using public hunters."[21]

Progress reports released by the cooperative project between 1964 and 1968 provided essential information on elk behavior and winter-range ecology. The final progress report, released in July 1968, described elk migration and distribution within the park and appeared to provide the information needed to make hunting an effective tool for elk control. The report also contained information that should have caused concern among Rocky Mountain's administration and scientific staff. First, "key" elk winter range was estimated at only 4,245 acres—far less than the 16,316-acre figure used by the Park Service.[22] Second, the report indicated that "heavy use of . . . browse species within elk concentration areas is evident . . . [and] approximately 60.6 percent of the key winter range areas with browse understories were rated as low vigor." Further, "45 percent of the aspen and 64 percent of the willow in the Park's major elk wintering areas had been heavily grazed."[23]

Most significantly, the report observed that the "Park [elk] herd is very prolific . . . approaching . . . the most prolific populations in Colorado." This statement was particularly alarming given that the study "estimated that winter ranges within the Park could only support from 400–600 elk, and elk numbers were approaching or exceeding that limit at the conclusion of the range investigations."[24] For park administrators and wildlife biologists, this should have been a clear warning that the elk problem was more complex than had been assumed. Since 1944 the Park Service had been physically removing elk from Rocky Mountain (from 1944 to 1961 by shooting and from 1962 to 1968 by trapping and relocation), and according to the park's best population estimates, the herd had been kept close to the estimated winter-range carrying capacity, averaging less than 600 per year. But damage was still occurring on Rocky Mountain's winter range, and the herd was still on the increase.

The explanation for this anomaly appeared on the final page of the 1968 report. The information released by the Park Service on elk numbers, the report concluded, were not as accurate as many believed. If anything, the agency had underestimated the elk population on the winter range. "The reliability of these counts," the report suggested, "is questionable." Good herd management demanded better population data. "One of the most urgent management needs concerning the Rocky Mountain National Park elk population," the report cautioned, "is that of obtaining reliable indicators of population levels."[25] This warning would return to haunt Rocky Mountain National Park over the next two decades. In the meantime, the Park Service decided that "enough data had been gathered . . . to recommend public hunting seasons outside the Park."[26]

In 1968 Rocky Mountain inaugurated its version of what Glen Cole, supervisory research biologist at Yellowstone, would christen in 1971 the natural regulation of elk.[27] The idea as developed by Cole was simple and appealing. It presumed that wildlife populations—particularly elk—were self-limiting, that population numbers were held down not just by natural predators like wolves or unnatural ones like man, but also by the limits of the available food supply and the natural culling effects of climatic extremes. Most importantly, the theory of natural regulation took it for granted that wildlife populations would reach equilibrium with their food supplies (the equivalent of carrying capacity) without damaging the vegetation base.[28]

Despite strong evidence of the failure of the park's herd to reach a natural balance with its food supply without damaging the vegetation base, Rocky Mountain National Park eagerly embraced natural regulation as the way to cap the elk population at ecological carrying capacity. In a 1968 policy statement on elk management, the park declared:

> It is the policy of the National Park Service to perpetuate animal life of the parks for their essential role in natural ecosystems . . . [and to] minimize the impact of modern man on the environment.
>
> In 1943, it was decided that these influences [of man] on the environment of the elk had so altered the ecosystem that natural regulations no longer limited the population. . . . [But today] the elk herd is . . . being allowed to fluctuate naturally with an eventual equilibrium with the forage supply expected.
>
> Public hunting outside the park is presently the preferred method [to facilitate natural regulation].[29]

On the basis of that policy and the 1962 MOU, Rocky Mountain National Park embarked on its experiment in natural regulation—an experiment similar to one being pursued in Yellowstone National Park, but with one important difference. Natural regulation of elk in Yellowstone, at least as outlined by Cole, relied neither on natural (wolves) nor unnatural (human) predators for success.[30] Elk numbers would reach a dynamic balance with the land through a series of iterations based on the natural and spontaneous adaptations of elk and vegetation to one another and the killing effects of drought, severe cold, and blizzards on sick and aged elk. In contrast, Rocky Mountain's experiment in natural regulation relied on hunting pressure outside the park to reinforce the culling effects of climatic extremes and the hoped-for natural equilibrium that would emerge between elk numbers and park vegetation.[31]

To monitor Rocky Mountain's experimental version of natural regulation, David Stevens, a wildlife biologist from the Montana Department of Fish, Wildlife, and Parks with extensive experience in Yellowstone, was brought in to head the park's small science staff. His experience with natural regulation in Yellowstone would be invaluable in monitoring Rocky Mountain's progress, and he understood the unique circumstances of Rocky Mountain's elk herd. Like the park's administrators, he believed that once the elk population reached equilibrium with the food supply, any additions to the herd would either succumb to weather extremes or simply migrate out of the park's protective boundaries.[32] The excess elk would then be harvested by hunters, ensuring the ecological health and sustainability of Rocky Mountain's winter range. All that was required was the agreement of the U.S. Forest Service and the Colorado Division of Wildlife.

Cooperation from Rocky Mountain's sister agencies came quickly. The Forest Service was eager to cull the large numbers of elk that were competing with domestic livestock for forage and in some cases damaging private fields. The agency was more than happy to step up hunting pressure along the park's eastern boundary. The Colorado Division of Wildlife was also glad to comply. Its biologists knew that the park's elk population was excessive, and they were familiar with the scenario being played out on Rocky Mountain's winter range. Pressure from property owners claiming elk depredation and from hunters demanding more elk permits gave extra incentive to the Division of Wildlife to lengthen the hunting season around Rocky Mountain and to issue more permits than ever before for the harvest of the park's unwanted elk.

Under the policy of natural regulation, the elk herds of Rocky Mountain have waned and waxed—although mostly the latter. The only factor slowing their increase has been hunting pressure from outside the park's boundaries. Published park estimates of the winter-range elk population show a gradual rise in herd numbers from a low of 500 in 1968 to 1,100 in 1979.[33] The park's estimates for 1980 to 1990 are less definitive. Only the raw data of visual counts are provided, with no attempts made to extrapolate from visual counts to actual population estimates. Based on annual counts and the informed opinions of park scientists, however, elk numbers on Rocky Mountain's winter range had increased to at least 1,600 by 1990. Tempering that estimate was Stevens's observation that "the total number of elk on the winter range in the park appears to have stabilized."[34] Stabilized or not, 1,600 head of elk on winter range was far more than had been present during the late 1930s and early 1940s, when overgrazing was endemic—and the number exceeded by 400 percent the initial estimates of the park's winter-range carrying capacity. It is true that Rocky Mountain's winter range was significantly expanded in 1962 with the acquisition of portions of Moraine Park. It is also clear that the removal of cattle from the park prior to 1962 enhanced the capacity of the winter range to support a larger elk herd.

In 1982 Thompson Hobbs added new complexity to the debate on Rocky Mountain's winter range with published findings from his doctoral research at the Department of Fishery and Wildlife Biology and the Natural Resources Ecology Lab at Colorado State University. Hobbs calculated winter-range carrying capacities to be well above the previous standard of 400 head. Basing his estimates on elk energy requirements for the winter seasons of 1976–1977 and 1977–1978, he calculated the winter-range carrying capacity to be 991 head for the first season and 1,481 head for the second.[35] If Hobbs's estimates were correct, Rocky Mountain's elk population in 1990 was as much as 60 percent or as little as 8 percent above carrying capacity. Assuming the latter figure is the most accurate, the park's program of natural regulation was right on target—a conclusion shared by Stevens and other park staff. But there are problems with this conclusion. From the perspective of the Colorado Division of Wildlife and the Roosevelt National Forest, the natural regulation of Rocky Mountain's elk herd had been a disastrous failure.

Originally the Division of Wildlife had agreed to increase hunting pressure along the park's eastern boundary as a means to trim Rocky Mountain's elk herd. The idea was simple. If hunting pressure could reduce elk numbers outside the park, then elk residing within the park would willingly migrate onto national forest lands to fill vacant habitat. In this manner, elk numbers within the park would be held in check and elk numbers outside the park would be maintained. But the experiment in natural regulation did not work. Today Division of Wildlife data indicate that the elk herd living outside the park's boundaries has been severely depleted. Years of heavy hunting pressure have brought the Roosevelt National Forest herd to its lowest level in years. Park elk that were supposed to have moved onto National Forest lands to fill empty habitat have not behaved as predicted. Instead of migrating en masse, most of them stayed within Rocky Mountain's boundaries. As a result, the Colorado Division of Wildlife drastically reduced elk hunting permits in all management units bordering the park beginning with the 1992 season. The agency is now considering suspending elk hunting for an indefinite period in those areas, pending recovery of the herd.[36]

The Division of Wildlife has effectively short-circuited the 1962 MOU upon which Rocky Mountain's experiment in natural regulation is based. Biologists at the Division of Wildlife readily acknowledge the serious elk problem facing the park, but their first responsibility is to rebuild the herd that was undone by natural regulation policy. Until that is accomplished, Gene Schoonveldt, senior big game biologist for the Colorado Division of Wildlife, has said, "Rocky Mountain is on its own—the National Park Service will have to put its own house in order."[37]

Putting its own house in order may be a challenge for Rocky Mountain National Park. The end of the MOU spells the end of hunting as a method of controlling the elk population. Between 1968 and 1979, for example, nearly 200 head of elk a year were harvested along the park's boundaries. Although many of those elk did not come from the Rocky Mountain herd, some did. Indeed, from the point of view of park scientists, "this rate of removal [200 head] has slowed the rate of increase in [elk] population and may be somewhat compensating for the loss of predators."[38] Assuming that this line of reasoning is valid, the park elk that might have been eliminated by hunting will now simply augment current numbers and further contribute to one of the "most prolific populations in Colorado."[39] But there is an even greater obstacle to the park putting its house in order. Persuasive evidence suggests that Rocky Mountain's winter-range elk population has not been kept in check under the regime of heavy hunting and natural regulation.

A 1989 Colorado Division of Wildlife study concluded that "the population [of elk in Estes Park] in the winter of 1981–1982 had exceeded carrying capacity of the range, *even with mild winter conditions,* and was reflected in lower calf weights."[40] Winter-range carrying capacity—at least based on Hobbs's liberal calculations—had, in fact, been exceeded a year earlier when George Bear, a Colorado Division of Wildlife biologist, had estimated the population of Rocky Mountain's winter-range elk herd to be as high as 1,641 head.[41] This figure contrasted sharply with Stevens's 1979 estimate of 1,100 head and even exceeded the record elk counts of the late 1930s and early 1940s. More significantly, the 1989 Division of Wildlife study estimated that the elk population on Rocky Mountain's winter range had swollen beyond 3,000 head by the winter of 1982–1983. Although the report failed to give more up-to-date population estimates, it did conclude that elk in 1989 "were having a definite effect on the plant community. Grasses and forbs outside fenced exclosures in Beaver Meadows were grazed to ground level in late winter and there was a noticeable lack of shrub or tree regeneration. Mature aspen trees are being severely damaged by elk feeding on bark."[42]

Contrary to the optimistic conclusion Stevens offered in his 1990 report, the elk population in Rocky Mountain had not stabilized within the limits of winter-range carrying capacity.[43] Indeed, Stevens had conceded in his 1982 report that the elk population had increased to 3,000 head and that "perhaps the population is exceeding what would be considered natural use levels."[44] This concession contrasts with Stevens's 1980 projection that park "ranges are nearing ecological carrying capacity, [and] the expected equilibrium may not be far from reality."[45] It is apparent that from 1980 to 1982, elk populations surpassed ecological carrying capacity and that equilibrium was left in the dust of an overstocked winter range. Stevens's later reports (through 1990) do not provide population estimates, but they do suggest that elk numbers on the winter range increased through 1984 and then leveled off and stabilized in subsequent years.

If Stevens's written observations from 1982 to 1990 are credible, then it is reasonable to conclude that the population estimate advanced by the Colorado Division of Wildlife in 1982 is still applicable. Indeed, testimony by biologists at both Rocky Mountain National Park and the Division of Wildlife point to the possibility that winter-range elk numbers may now exceed 3,000 head.[46] That figure is double the estimate Stevens made in 1990, but it is in many ways more consistent with the evidence available for Rocky Mountain's winter range. There is also reason to doubt the validity of Hobbs's estimates on winter-range carrying capacity. His calculations are based on the full use by elk of all available winter-range habitat. But elk prefer some areas to others, and the actual winter range that is used for feeding may be significantly smaller than the potential winter range fed into Hobbs's calculations.

In the final analysis, however, the calculus of population numbers and the vagaries of carrying capacity dwindle in importance against the reality of what elk have done to Rocky Mountain National Park. If their numbers have stabilized within the park's carrying capacity as Stevens suggests, then natural harmony and vegetal health should be evident on the landscape. If they have not—if elk numbers exceed carrying capacity by 100 percent or more (depending on what real carrying capacity is)—then the evidence should be even more conspicuous on the face of the land.[47]

THE LASTING LEGACY OF ELK

Rocky Mountain's elk problem is relatively recent and to a large extent has been obscured by the historical presence of cattle in Estes Park. Livestock grazing was the predominant influence on the ecological condition and environmental health of Rocky Mountain from 1880 to 1930.[48] In fact, most ecological studies of the Rocky Mountain West assume that grazing damage is a phenomenon attributable exclusively to the raising of domestic stock on western wild lands. "Cattle and sheep grazing," observed a recent U.S. Fish and Wildlife Service publication, "impacts intermountain basin, subalpine, and montane wetland areas and mountain meadows throughout the Rocky Mountain West. Major effects include vegetation damage, reduction, and removal; soil compaction and erosion; and potable water degradation from fecal contamination. Grazing along riparian wetlands can also result in . . . destruction of riverbanks.'[49]

Ironically, the effects ascribed to livestock grazing appear similar to the environmental problems now plaguing Rocky Mountain, even though livestock have been absent from most of the park for almost three-quarters of a century (the exceptions being parts of Moraine Park until 1962 and the Never Summer Ranch until 1975). Assuming that the Park Service is correct in its estimate that the Rocky Mountain elk herd has stabilized and is in equilibrium with its environment, vegetation conditions in the park should be superior to those seen under a grazing regime of cattle and sheep. In fact, Rocky Mountain's 1968 policy statement on elk management asserts unequivocally that the success of natural regulation of the elk population on the winter range is to be measured "by studying the reaction of climax vegetation to the grazing influence."[50] The ecological condition of winter-range vegetation is, and properly should be, the final arbiter of the success or failure of natural regulation.

The effects of elk and cattle on winter-range vegetation are nearly indistinguishable. Both have a strong preference for "wet meadow and aspen types" because of "the relatively high abundance of graminoids [grasses] and shrubs," and both are capable of overgrazing native ranges.[51] Although no scientific surveys of winter-range conditions were done prior to 1915, when the park was founded, observers such as Enos Mills and Martin Estes could see the effect of too many cattle on Rocky Mountain's meadows and wetlands. By 1900 it was painfully evident to many area residents that chronic over-grazing had mowed valley vegetation to the ground and left wet areas trampled and barren.[52] The gradual elimination of livestock from Rocky Mountain between 1915 and 1930, however, relieved grazing pressure on valley meadows and aspen groves and allowed winter-range vegetation to begin its recovery to presettlement conditions.

Simultaneous with the phasing out of livestock, the park pursued a de facto policy of natural regulation of elk until 1944. During the 1930s the

large elk herd caused widespread and—in the eyes of most scientific observers—devastating effects on winter-range vegetation. Fred Packard, the
Civilian Conservation Corps wildlife biologist, observed in 1942 that elk in
Rocky Mountain National Park were the primary *faunal* influence on aspen,
and that the ability of aspen stands to reproduce themselves was greatly
limited by elk grazing on seedlings and sucker sprouts. Moreover, elk chewing
on bark, thus girdling trees, and rubbing their antlers against tree trunks was
a primary cause of aspen die-off. Packard described how fungus diseases
entered through wounds in the bark of otherwise healthy trees and left
once-vigorous aspen clones decadent and dying. "The few elk re-introduced
into the park area," he noted, "had multiplied to about twelve hundred by
1940; it is believed that the concentration of these elk on their restricted
winter range near Estes Park is responsible for the magnitude of the damage
to the aspen in that region."[53]

Describing the damage, Packard was quite graphic:

> The nature of the condition is well shown in Beaver Meadow, central
> most of the narrow valleys utilized by elk in winter. This is a park of
> grassy meadows and some two-and-one-half miles long, tapering from
> one mile to perhaps three hundred yards in width. A small stream
> meanders down the park through a border of willows; the southern
> margin of the meadow is conifer-clad moraine, with a belt of tall aspen
> parallel along its foot. . . . The trunk of every aspen in this meadow is
> heavily scarred as high as the elk can reach, and no branches survive below
> that height. There is almost no reproduction. The trees bordering the
> meadows are dead or dying by the hundreds. . . . It is almost certain that
> in comparatively few years all of these aspens will have died. . . . On April
> 26, 1939, two hundred and forty elk were counted in this one meadow.[54]

Packard was amazingly accurate in his forecast. Today visitors must search far
and wide to find a living aspen tree in Beaver Meadows, not to mention robust
and thriving aspen stands.[55] But more than aspen succumbed to elk grazing
in the park's de facto experiment with natural regulation.

In 1959 Leslie Gysel, a wildlife and fisheries professor at Michigan State
University, reflected on the history of Rocky Mountain National Park and
the role that elk had played in transforming the park's natural vegetation since
1930. "Most visitors in the park who pass by Horseshoe Park and Beaver
Meadow," he wrote,

> would never realize that these extensive grass areas with a few willows
> (*Salix* spp.) have undergone major changes. Old residents reported that

a large part of these areas were once occupied by willows. . . . It was noted in subsequent wildlife reports (1934, 1935) that willow was heavily browsed by elk. In 1939, Dixon reported that the destruction of willow in the winter range had been most marked, especially in Beaver Meadow where 285 elk were counted at one time.[56]

To assess the long-term impact of elk on winter-range conditions, Gysel revisited exclosures that had been built during the 1930s and 1940s. For the Beaver Meadows exclosures, he measured 70 and 15 percent willow cover within their protected areas. Outside the exclosures, he recorded no willow cover in adjacent unprotected control plots. In Horseshoe Park, he found 45 percent willow cover in the exclosure and no willow cover in the control plot. He also reported that willows growing in the exclosures were between six and ten feet tall. Where willows could still be found on open, unprotected range, they were less than four feet tall and showed signs of declining health. Gysel concluded that "without protection from elk, the willow are apparently going out in the grass-willow transition zones."[57]

Wet meadows and moderately moist grasslands were also subject to the depredations of too many elk. Although not utilized as heavily as aspen and willow stands for winter range, grassy areas were still preferred by elk as grazing sites.[58] Buttery's 1955 analysis of park range conditions in the aftermath of years of heavy elk use shows a pattern of abuse and destruction in the meadows. He found winter-range grasslands in low seral condition, an ecological state far below optimal plant community composition and productivity. "*Danthoni[a] parryi*, a desirable species," he observed, "was found to be almost entirely lacking and was replaced mainly by *Bouteloua gracilis*, which is . . . an indicator of a lower stage of succession." Wet meadows showed similar signs of overgrazing, including drying soil conditions and invading, low-successional plant species. "Findings on the Beaver Meadow and Horseshoe Park areas," Buttery suggested, "indicate that in the past they have, as a whole, been damaged to a considerable extent, particularly along Fall River in Horseshoe Park." Further, he stated, "the fact that as a whole, these concentration areas are in fair range condition and progressing toward a better condition is due, no doubt, to the introduction of the elk-deer reduction program in December, 1944."[59]

By all accounts, the vegetation of Rocky Mountain's winter range fared well during the decades of active elk population control. The same cannot be said for the years since 1968, particularly the 1980s and early 1990s, when elk population may have exceeded three thousand head. For better or worse, the policy of natural regulation has ruled the ecology of the range tenaciously.[60] Bitter lessons learned from the past have been forgotten or cast aside by administrators and scientists eager to mold Rocky Mountain into a place where natural processes, rather than humans, shape life and landscapes. The environmental legacy of almost a quarter-century of natural regulation is dismal at best and distressing at worst. Winter ranges in the park that were initially given a reprieve from cattle in 1915 and later rescued from elk in 1944 are neither stable nor improving ecologically.[61] A population explosion of elk is changing the face of Rocky Mountain in ways and to a degree that cattle never did.

The worsening fate of aspen tells part of the story of natural regulation during modern times. Beginning in the late 1970s, a series of academic studies on Rocky Mountain's aspen forests warned of imminent danger. Frederic Nichols showed that elk grazing of sucker sprouts was a major cause of the decadence and dying of winter-range aspen stands.[62] Charles Olmsted reinforced Nichols' findings when he concluded that "the level of browsing utilization compatible with [aspen] stand maintenance is relatively low (approximately 30%)." In the Rocky Mountains, he wrote, "aspen reproduction is almost entirely dependent on the vegetative propagation of suckers from roots." But, he continued, "the utilization of aspen on this range appears to be equal to or more severe than that reported [from other national parks]." Successful aspen regeneration in Rocky Mountain National Park, Olmsted stated, depended on "some means of reducing browsing pressure."[63]

Olmsted's findings were alarming, given that aspen utilization on Rocky Mountain's winter range greatly exceeded 30 percent. Park data for 1969–1978—when the elk population was believed to be less than 1,000 head—showed aspen utilization levels averaging 69 percent, "with 48% of the young trees being severely hedged in 1978."[64] Aspen stands could neither reproduce nor survive under such an intensive grazing regime. But for the purposes of natural regulation, the loss of aspen was not necessarily a violation of natural processes. Some Park Service ecologists argued that the disappearance of aspen in protected areas like Rocky Mountain was permissible because the resulting landscape would be a "zootic climax"—a natural vegetation community created by the natural influences of a native species, elk.[65]

But arguing away, or simply dismissing, the "aspen problem" by suggesting that its causes were "natural" overlooked—or denied—the persuasive and contrary ecological evidence at hand for the central Rockies. The conclusions of Alan A. Beetle, a University of Wyoming plant ecologist who studied the aspen of northern Colorado and Wyoming, matched those of Olmsted: aspen had been a major component of the Rocky Mountain landscape since the closing of the Pleistocene era several thousand years earlier.[66] Olmsted, bolstered by Beetle's data, held firm. He insisted that "the decline and potential disappearance of these aspen stands on the [park's] winter range [due to elk] does not seem consonant with either natural ecosystem processes or the Park management goal of the maintenance of pristine ecosystems." Olmsted also warned that if aspen disappeared from the park's winter range, it was unlikely that they would reestablish themselves naturally.[67]

Olmsted's prophecy is coming true on Rocky Mountain's winter range. Aspen are disappearing from overuse by elk. Even worse, stands that were eliminated in the past show no signs of recovery. According to Park Service records, "aspen in 1930 occupied considerably more area on the east side of the Park than it does today."[68] Annual Park Service field reports from 1968 through 1990 attest to the downward spiral of aspen in Rocky Mountain:

> Aspen resprouts are heavily used . . . on key elk winter range. Some stands are deteriorating and will probably disappear within several years [1968].

> Aspen . . . heavily used . . . 84% [1971].

> Aspen in Upper Beaver Meadow and Horseshoe Park are deteriorating in condition and in time will disappear [1973].

> Aspen plants are in poor condition [1977].

> In Moraine Park . . . days use per acre [on aspen] increased from 20 to 124, or a 520% increase [1981].

> The aspen stands continue to be the vegetation type most severely impacted by [elk] use [1984].

> The trend is still toward the deterioration of the aspen stands as use continues to increase [1987].

> Under present browsing pressures, most of the lower elevation [winter range] aspen stands can be expected to eventually disappear [1988].

> Elk browsing may be the primary factor in [the] ultimate loss of the aspen stand [1990].[69]

Today the evidence of aspen's decline under the regime of natural regulation is conspicuous on the lower elevations of Rocky Mountain's east side. Mature trees in virtually every stand in the winter range are scarred by elk antlers and fatally infected with fungus disease. Seedlings that might have replaced the dead and dying aspen are grazed to the ground. Indicative of this decline is an aspen-ringed meadow that once greeted tourists near the Fall River entrance to the park. In the late 1970s bull elk invaded the grove and destroyed trees and seedlings. Today not a single living aspen remains in the

A visually striking sign of heavy elk use of aspen is the existence of a distinct browse line, exemplified in the top photograph of a dying aspen stand on the northern perimeter of Moraine Park. The "browse" line is the result of the elk consuming all leaf and stem material within their reach. In this case, the browse line approximates the arm's reach of a tall person (top photograph). The browse line, however, is only the outward sign of a more profound grazing effect. The interior of heavily browsed aspen stands reveals severely hedged aspen suckers, badly scarred tree trunks, and an almost universal deterioration of individual trees and understory vegetation (bottom photograph). Aspen stands undergoing this degree of grazing use are fated to disappear from the landscape. Photographs by author (June 1993).

Death of an aspen on the winter range. Drawing by Shannon Lenz-Wall.

small meadow. Farther to the south, on the hillsides below Bierstadt Lake, the most extensive aspen stands remaining in the park are decadent and dying from elk abuse. Near the helicopter landing site in the upper reaches of Beaver Meadows, the aspen stands mapped during the 1980s have disappeared. Ironically, the only healthy and reproducing stand of aspen in the winter range is in an elk-proof exclosure built at the far western end of Beaver Meadows. When the exclosure was built in the early 1960s, aspen thrived across a much broader expanse of the park's winter range. Now, the only evidence of aspen beyond the exclosure's perimeter is a handful of fungus-infected trees.[70]

Willow stands, wet meadows, and dry grasslands in Rocky Mountain's winter range have been similarly affected by the policy of natural regulation. The continuously expanding herd of elk has impoverished some of the biologically richest and most diverse ecosystems in the park. Unlike the visually conspicuous decline of aspen, however, evidence of the environ-

Top photograph shows large stand of aspen at the upper end of Beaver Meadows. The stand is fully protected from elk grazing by a surrounding elk-proof fence erected in 1963. Vegetation in the protected understory is dense and highly diverse. Bottom photograph shows a side view of the same aspen stand. The protected aspen can be seen in the background. In the foreground, the dead and dying remnants of unprotected aspen are evident. Heavy elk grazing and elk-induced fungal disease have virtually eliminated aspen from outside of the fenced perimeter and greatly diminished the density and diversity of ground vegetation. Photographs by author (June 1993).

Top photograph was taken within an elk-proof exclosure erected in 1962 and located toward the upper end of Beaver Meadows. In the far background of the protected site is a healthy stand of aspen. In front of the aspen is a ribbon of tall willows. In the foreground are a number of wet meadow species including cow parsnip (represented by dried stalks). Cow parsnip is a favored food of elk and is rare outside of the exclosure. Bottom photograph shows the same exclosure in the background. In the foreground, widely spaced alders are all that is left of a riparian community that once contained an abundance of willow and cow parsnip. Photographs by author (June 1993).

Top photograph shows hedging effect of elk grazing on willows in lower Horseshoe Park. Not only has grazing pressure drastically reduced the presence of willow, but plants that should be five/ten feet in height are now barely taller than the surrounding grasses.. Photograph on facing page shows a similar browsing effect on aspen at the edge of Moraine Park. Like willows, aspen suckers invariably die under such heavy grazing use. Photographs by author (June 1993).

mental decay of these other plant communities comes exclusively from verbal and written reports. Part of the evidence is anecdotal. Park naturalists stationed in Rocky Mountain's Kawuneeche Valley have reported that elk have destroyed large willow stands in recent years. Grossly simplified plant communities, composed of only a few grazing-resistant species, have replaced the biologically diverse and complex willow stands. Park biologists have dismissed the loss because they do not consider willows the primary food source for elk and, most importantly, because they consider willows successional anyway.[71]

The most telling evidence of environmental degradation comes directly from David Stevens, the biologist in charge of monitoring Rocky Mountain's experiment in natural regulation. Since 1968 Stevens's annual field reports have detailed mounting levels of elk use of willows, meadows, and grasslands and have documented vegetation destruction that far exceeds the historical impact of livestock on Estes Park. As early as 1969 Stevens reported that the ecological results of natural regulation were anything but satisfactory: "On

the xeric grassland areas utilization remained high. . . . The xeric grassland areas continue to remain in a dis-climax successional stage primarily as a result of heavy elk use . . . [and] with the present elk population densities on these ranges, normal succession will not progress to climax. Willow utilization remained high with 68% of the plants heavily hedged and 78% utilization.'[72] In laymen's terms, elk were still grazing the park's grasslands at record levels. Weedy species were replacing the natural diversity of grasses and flowering plants and preventing the recovery of overgrazed grasslands. Finally, elk were consuming willow with as much rapacity as they were devouring grass.

The record of natural regulation has steadily worsened. Again, park records[73] provide a graphic account of the ecological effects of a mushrooming elk herd:

1975—Willow is . . . being eliminated on some sites due to heavy elk use.

1977—On easternmost willow transect, the willow is almost gone.

1980—In elk days use per acre, a substantial increase overall was noted on grassland and meadow types.

1981—Willow utilization increased considerably. On the meadow sites, a major increase in elk days use per acre was recorded, from 57 in 1980 to 107 this year.

1982—The meadow areas in Moraine Park showed very heavy use. . . . There now appears to be a lack of replacement for the plants being lost. This is probably the result of grazing pressure.

1983—[Dry grasslands] indicate some continued decline. . . . [Wet meadows] experienced the largest increase in use since 1968 as a result of the increasing elk population . . . [and are moving] toward more xeric conditions. Two stands [of willows] in Moraine Park and Upper Beaver Meadows declined quite drastically.

1984—86% estimated utilization [on dry grasslands] . . . and 76% utilization of the [wet meadow] plants . . . [represent] just about the maximum possible on these sites. [Willow] utilization remained high at 74% . . . [and] of the 25 plants tagged on the transect in 1968, only 6 remain alive and they are in very poor condition.

1985—Two of the five [willow] stands studied are being eliminated rapidly [by elk]. . . . Overall utilization increased to over 86%.

1986—Use of grass is about at the maximum that is available (85%). . . . This level of use has resulted in a zootic disclimax. [Tufted hairgrass] has just about disappeared from [Moraine Park]. Two tagged willow plants died since last year.

1987—[Grassland utilization] was about maximum . . . estimated to average 82%. The meadow type continues to receive the heaviest use. The degree of hedging [of willows] . . . has also started back up.

1988—Estimated utilization of the [dry grassland] plants also remained high at 88 percent. Estimated [meadow] utilization . . . has now reached 79 percent. [Willow] stands continue to decline.

1989—Estimated utilization of the [dry grassland] plants remained high at 92 percent. [Wet meadow] type continues to show increases in elk use. . . . Utilization . . . has now reached 80%. [Willow] use [has increased] from 78 percent in 1968 to 81 percent this year. . . . [The] level of use . . . [is] too high over the long term for willow, and several of the stands continue to decline.

1990—Estimated utilization of the [dry grassland] plants remained high at 93%. [Wet meadow] utilization . . . has now reached 88 percent. Two stands [of willow] are especially close to being eliminated [by elk].

The park's record on natural regulation speaks for itself. Dry grasslands have not moved toward climax conditions—the state in which the numbers and types of species in a plant community are stable and optimal for the environment—but have deteriorated more each year into weedy plant communities that bear little resemblance to what existed prior to non-Indian settlement. Wet meadows have been hit so hard by elk that once-abundant native species, such as tufted hairgrass, are being replaced at an escalating pace by Canadian thistles. Willow stands, once so prominent on Rocky Mountain's winter range, are fading from the landscape. Nowhere is this change more dramatic than in Horseshoe Park, where an elk exclosure from the 1960s guarded until recently the last remnant of an expansive willow stand.[74] More alarmingly, park records dating from 1989 have documented severe elk impacts on willow communities lying outside Rocky Mountain's winter range. Alpine willow stands are now declining, the result of growing numbers of elk being forced to winter above tree line in the never-ending search for food. Even subalpine willow stands are beginning to exhibit the classic symptoms of excessive elk grazing.[75] Worse yet, measurements and reports by Stevens and others show ominous signs of increasing bare ground and erosion in the park's winter range.[76] Elk have begun a sort of desertification of an environment that until very recently was the garden spot of the central Rocky Mountains.

Most disturbing of all is that the pace of the destruction of Rocky Mountain's winter range quickens almost daily despite the corrective mechanisms built into the park's long-standing policy on elk management. "The

Top and bottom photographs show contrast between grass density and vigor inside and outside of an elk-proof exclosure erected in 1962 and located toward the upper end of Beaver Meadows. Top photograph shows evidence of heavy elk grazing on the right side of the exclosure. Note the dense aspen in the back of the exclosure and its absence outside of the exclosure. Bottom photograph shows dense and vigorous grass in the protected background and severely grazed grass in the unprotected foreground. Differences in species composition is strikingly evident in ungrazed versus grazed sides. Photographs by author (June 1993).

One small piece of Rocky Mountain's unraveling winter range is the impending loss of the park's only substantial stand of cottonwood trees. Perched along the edges of an active spring in Moraine Park, the cottonwood stand (top photograph) is dying as mature trees topple and as replacement suckers are grazed to the ground by elk (bottom photograph). What could be an invaluable interpretive stop for Rocky Mountain's visitors is instead a nagging reminder of neglect and mismanagement. Photographs by author (June 1993).

reaction of climax vegetation to the grazing influence" is the standard by which the performance of natural regulation is supposed to be measured, yet vegetation each day recedes further from climax and moves steadily toward decline and decay.[77] By some inscrutable logic, the loss of aspen, the destruction of willows, the overgrazing of wet meadows, and the deterioration of dry grasslands are not sufficient evidence to trigger the ameliorative steps mandated by Rocky Mountain's elk management policy: "If the present program is not successful in holding the elk population in check, and damage to the park ecosystem exceeds tolerance levels, resumption of control in the park will be necessary. Other factors that may require control within the park would be a complete closure to hunting in the Estes Valley."[78]

If the destruction of the park's winter range has not exceeded "tolerance levels," then what conditions would? The Colorado Division of Wildlife will limit elk hunting in the Estes Valley in 1992 and possibly suspend it in the near future—an action that by itself is sufficient to reactivate elk control in Rocky Mountain. But the park's administration is not planning to resume elk control; it is still as committed to natural regulation as it was in 1968. Sadly, that commitment is affecting more than aspen, willows, meadows, and grasslands. The loss of the park's winter range is playing havoc with the welfare of wildlife. A number of very visible and popular animals are being edged out of Rocky Mountain by an aggressively expanding elk herd.

BEAVERS, WILLOWS, AND ELK

The consequences of elk fecundity and overgrazed winter range have sent ecological shock waves through many of the wildlife populations of Rocky Mountain National Park. The large numbers of elk in the park have turned the natural world of bighorn sheep topsy-turvy. The presence of the elk has altered the sheep's migration patterns and restricted their usable habitat, putting a major attraction of the park at considerable risk. As early as 1941, wildlife biologists were aware of habitat competition between native ungulates. "One example of this," observed Harold Ratcliff, a wildlife biologist with the National Park Service,

> is indicated at Rocky Mountain National Park where the elk are crowded back on areas formerly used almost exclusively by the bighorns. As a result of this competition for forage by the two species, the bighorns have been forced to remain on higher wind-swept areas . . . whereas formerly they migrated in winter to lower elevations . . . which are now used extensively by the elk. . . . The lower elevation ranges are now so badly

overgrazed that in many instances the elk themselves are wintering above timberline . . . using forage badly needed by the bighorns."[79]

The ptarmigan, a member of the grouse family and a resident of the park's high country, also appears to be suffering from the expanding Rocky Mountain elk herd. As elk numbers continue to exceed winter-range carrying capacity, and as alpine and subalpine willow stands consequently deteriorate, ptarmigan habitat and population are endangered. That conflict was first suggested by David Stevens in 1980, when he predicted that "reduction in the willow habitat on the alpine would probably affect white-tailed ptarmigan populations."[80] A decade later, he reformulated his prediction in greater detail and with more certainty: "We presently hypothesize that heavy use of willow by elk in early winter and early spring constrains ptarmigan breeding densities by reducing amount of food (willow buds) available to ptarmigan in late winter during the early breeding period. . . . [Ptarmigan populations] may be . . . depressed excessively when their habitats are heavily used by elk.[81]

As significant as the effects of elk on bighorn sheep and ptarmigan may be, the most pronounced and ecologically damaging legacy of the Rocky Mountain herd is the loss of beaver from the park's winter range. Prior to permanent European settlement, beaver were abundant in Rocky Mountain. "A numerous beaver population," Enos Mills observed, "led trappers into this territory probably as early as 1841."[82] But by 1890 too many trappers, too many settlers, and too many cattle had virtually eliminated beaver from Estes Park. When the area became a national park, however, beaver had the chance to recover both lost numbers and lost habitat.

Data on beaver recovery are sparse and incomplete, but evidence suggests that the population in the park peaked just as elk reached and then exceeded the carrying capacity of the winter range. In 1926, for example, a population census taken along Cow Creek and Roaring Fork rivers found 112 beaver.[83] Fourteen years later, just as elk were beginning to ravage Rocky Mountain's winter range, Fred Packard took a similar census along the same drainages. He found only 27 beaver in residence, indicating a possible population decline of nearly 500 percent. Unlike the 1926 study, however, the 1940 census (not published until 1947) also covered all of the major drainages of Rocky Mountain National Park. In total, Packard counted a population of 1,865 beaver in the park.[84] Because of the magnitude and scope of Packard's later survey, the comparison between it and the 1926 census is less instructive than the comparison between it and subsequent counts on identical key winter-range drainages in 1964, 1980, and 1981.

Beaver at home in early Rocky Mountain National Park. Drawing by Shannon Lenz-Wall.

Packard's 1940 beaver count on the winter range showed an estimated population of 890—a population that in all probability was already on a downward slide.[85] Twenty-four years later, when scientists from Rocky Mountain visited the Big Thompson drainage, where Packard had counted 315 beavers, they found only 102 of the animals. Sixteen years later in 1980, park staff revisited the area and reported only 12 beaver remaining. More significantly, they found only 108 beaver for all of the key winter-range drainages that Packard had studied—a decline in overall winter-range population of almost 900 percent.[86] Despite alleged methodological differences between the 1940 and 1980 studies, park scientists conceded that "generally it appears that there has been a major decline in beaver in the areas surveyed."[87] In 1981, when park scientists repeated the winter-range census, they found that beaver numbers had remained steady or declined slightly except on the Fall River drainage, where beaver numbers appeared to have increased significantly, from 30 in 1980 to 105 in 1981.[88] Apart from this unusually large jump in population—explainable only by a counting error or a remarkable immigration of animals—the beaver population had changed very little, as expected. Since 1981 the park has not conducted winter-range beaver counts, but there is no evidence to suggest that the beaver population has staged a recovery. Observations by park wildlife biologists strongly suggest that Rocky Mountain's beaver population has merely held its own over the past decade.[89]

In contrast to Rocky Mountain's stable yet anemic beaver population, urban areas along Colorado's Front Range are facing an explosion in beaver numbers. West Denver and Fort Collins are plagued with more beaver than their residents and their tamed landscapes can handle. Along sections of the Cache la Poudre River that pass through Fort Collins, for example, beaver have become pests, harvesting aspen, cottonwoods, and willows that line the river and make up the artificial landscapes of city homes. Because beaver are protected from trapping within the city limits, their numbers keep escalating and residents' complaints keep mounting. Even in the surrounding rural areas in Larimer County, where beaver are not protected, their numbers are increasing faster than landowners can control.[90] What is happening in urban and rural Colorado is merely the tip of an iceberg. Nationwide, beaver numbers have risen dramatically from an estimated low of 100,000 in 1920 to over 15 million today.[91]

Ironically, fifty miles upstream at the headwaters of the Cache la Poudre River, in the very heart of Rocky Mountain National Park, beaver are faring poorly. Valleys like Beaver Meadows no longer have active beaver lodges. Despite the park's role as a biosphere reserve to provide "a standard against which the effect of man's impact on his environment can be measured," something has happened to make Rocky Mountain a less attractive beaver habitat than the urban environment of Fort Collins—or, for that matter, the vast rural and urban environments of North America where beaver populations have steadily climbed. That something is thousands of elk grazing willows and aspen to near extinction on the park's winter range.

Willows and aspen are part of the beaver's diet. They are also the building materials beaver use to dam streams and construct their lodges. Packard, in his studies of Rocky Mountain National Park, observed that the

> lack of aspen available for food and building material may hamper occupation of some otherwise habitable region. However, wherever willow grows abundantly near streams, the beaver accept that plant as a satisfactory substitute for aspen. This national park [Rocky Mountain] is unusual in the number of its colonies that have been developed around a dependence upon willow, few of them being primarily dependent upon aspen, as is often the case elsewhere.[92]

Willow, a primary food and building material for Rocky Mountain's beaver, is conspicuously missing from the streambanks of the Big Thompson as it passes through the lower reaches of Moraine Park (top photograph). Alder is the only visible shrubby species in the picture. Because of the absence of willow and beaver, the Park Service has installed artificial "beaver" dams (bottom photograph) as a means to maintain the meadow's high water table. Although artificial dams offer a technical solution to meadow dessication, they are poor substitutes for the restoration of willows and beaver to Moraine Park. Photographs by author (June 1993).

Dependence on willows has given the beaver in Rocky Mountain (at least prior to natural regulation) an edge on beaver that rely on aspen elsewhere. Generally the harvesting of aspen results in the exhaustion of aspen stands, forcing beaver to abandon their colonies and search elsewhere for food and wood. But when beaver rely on willows, a different situation is created. Because willows thrive in areas with high water tables and because water tables rise when beavers build dams, harvesting willows creates conditions favorable for more willow growth. In fact, studies of beaver ponds have shown that willow production is actually accelerated by beaver harvesting.[93]

The relationship between beaver and willows, however, was never so immutable as to be immune to all disruptions. As early as 1940, Packard warned that elk posed a serious threat to the park's winter-range beaver colonies:

> A serious problem, especially on streams in the vicinity of Estes Park, is the competitive effect of deer and elk on their winter range upon the supply of aspen and willow. About 1,200 elk are in the park, and many of them concentrate near the mountain meadows in winter. At that season they habitually chew the bark from the aspens, and the scars they make provide conditions ideal for the spread of several fungal diseases through the groves, leading to the eventual death of the trees. In addition, the elk . . . eat willow . . . [producing] a noticeable decrease in the beaver's food supply, which is especially conspicuous in Moraine Park.[94]

Prior to the population explosion of elk—even prior to the troubling signs observed by Packard in 1940—Moraine Park was home to large numbers of beaver. Their lodges dotted the valley landscape, creating small ponds at random and changing intervals along the slow-flowing Big Thompson River that bisected its considerable length. Over decades, as sedimentation filled in the ponds, beaver harvested the next generation of mature willow and built new dams, continuing the natural cycle of wetland rejuvenation. In this manner Moraine Park maintained its wild and diverse character, keeping alive a crucial element of the Rocky Mountain ecosystem.

Human settlement greatly affected the wetland cycle, as farmers drained portions of the valley, planted hay crops, and erected buildings.[95] But people did not eliminate beaver from Moraine Park. It was elk that finally ended the cycle of rejuvenation as the management regime of natural regulation took effect. Before beaver could harvest the next generation of mature willow stems, elk desperate for winter forage consumed them. Even the aspen growing along the valley fringes were devoured. Without those building materials and the food they provided, the beaver had to abandon Moraine Park.

Of the 315 beaver counted on the Big Thompson in 1940, a sizeable number made their home in Moraine Park.[96] Twenty-four years later, that population had dwindled to 102 for all of the Big Thompson, with only a small fraction actually residing within Moraine Park. In 1980—as the elk population soared toward an estimated 3,000 head—only 12 beaver could be found on the Big Thompson. None were left in Moraine Park.[97] Without beaver, the ponds disappeared, lowering the park's water table and dooming those willows that had survived overgrazing by elk. As the willows disappeared, elk attacked the lush understory of grasses and wildflowers, transforming the collage of meadow grasses and wildflowers into weedy, desiccated expanses. In the end, the mountain stream that had once meandered like a silver thread across the wetland's surface cut into drying soil, leaving in its wake exposed and deepening vertical banks devoid of vegetation.

The natural rhythms of restoration and renewal have been broken in far too many of the willow patches and wet meadows of Rocky Mountain National Park. The victim has been the lifeblood of the park—the innumerable wetlands that initially qualified Rocky Mountain as a biosphere reserve and established it as a standard for measuring man's effect on unprotected environments. The lesson from Moraine Park is instructional for all of Rocky Mountain: elk in unnatural numbers, in an environment disconnected from its natural rhythms and regulations, have rendered the populations of other species no less unnatural. The lesson is especially applicable to the park's winter range, where beaver no longer build their dams in historic numbers in the shadow of towering peaks. The story of Moraine Park is a tale of ecological harmony turned upside down, of a biosphere reserve gone astray despite the best intentions of people and the best designs of public policy.

Measuring the ecological costs of natural regulation to Rocky Mountain National Park entails more than a count of beavers or, for that matter, an inventory of ptarmigan, bighorn sheep, willow communities, wet meadows, aspen groves, and dry grasslands. Lost in the impoverishment of the park's landscape is the vitality and complexity of life called biological diversity. To the extent that the term means simply the number of species present, the loss to the park has been minimal and in no way attributable to elk. Indeed, grizzly bears and wolves faded from the Rocky Mountain scene for precisely the same reason elk populations exploded in the mid- and late twentieth century: the undoing of naturalness by the pervasive presence of the human hand.[98]

But biological diversity involves much more than the numbers of species residing on a landscape. It encompasses such things as genetic variation within species; the dispersal patterns of populations of species; the types, numbers, and distributions of plant and animal communities; the mix and richness of species that make up particular communities; and the kinds, structures, and relative abundance of the physical habitats in which plants and animals dwell. Rocky Mountain National Park is *ecologically* important because of the uniqueness of its biological diversity, because the mixture of species, communities, and habitats that brings its valley and mountain landscapes to life is not replicable anywhere else on Earth. Similarities may exist among forest and grassland ecosystems in the central and southern Rocky Mountains, but the infinite ways in which geology, soils, climate, and latitude combine preclude duplication of the most important expressions of local diversity.[99] That is why Rocky Mountain National Park was selected as a biosphere reserve. It is also why the unchecked expansion of elk is so troubling.

Aspen, willows, beaver, and ptarmigan may not be threatened with extinction in Rocky Mountain National Park, but the diversity that accompanies those species and their communities is most certainly threatened with decadence and disruption. As willows disappear, as beavers cease their wetland renewal projects, and as communities of aspen, wet meadows, and dry grasslands simplify and contract, the richness of life in Rocky Mountain diminishes. Habitats disappear from the landscape, numbers and types of communities decline, and the species mix and richness of those communities diminish. Fewer wetlands and aspen groves mean far fewer environments in which highly diverse collages of plants and animals can flourish. And as overall landscape diversity diminishes, fewer rather than more species stand out in the valleys and on the mountain sides. The total number of species remains static, but ecologically the park is different, more akin to the monocultures that humans create than the wild medleys spun by nature.

Elk in numbers that are neither natural nor naturally regulated are diminishing the variety and vitality of life in Rocky Mountain National Park. On this point the evidence is compelling. This does not mean, of course, that elk are bad and that beaver or some other species is better and to be preferred. It only means that current ratios of elk to beaver and other critical species are far from natural and that with every passing day the ratios skew increasingly in favor of elk—a consequence of the park's human-impacted environment, not a reflection of the poetry of natural regulation. Yet the threat to the park's physical and biological uniqueness involves more than elk devouring winter range and driving out beaver. Fire as much as elk lies at the heart of the unraveling ecology of Rocky Mountain.

CHAPTER 3

Landscapes of Fire

Rocky Mountain National Park is a geologically dynamic landscape. Primal forces have thrust mountain peaks skyward, and the erosive forces of nature have slowly begun to tame jagged peaks and soften rugged alpine terrain. Wind, water, and glaciers, the latter two propelled by the forces of gravity down steep gradients, have carved valley bottoms, reduced mountain slopes, molded ranges of low-lying moraines, and forged grass-laden saddles and rounded hilltops. These landscape features, the product of millions of years of uplift and erosion, have persisted relatively unchanged over recent millennia and will likely continue to do so for several millennia to come.

Geological forces, however, have sculpted only the nonliving surfaces of Rocky Mountain, the skeletal materials of mountains and valleys upon which generations of vegetation have attached themselves and flourished. The vegetal patterns that clothe Rocky Mountain and give life to its granite surfaces are the result of factors more immediate and more conspicuous in their effects. Permanent human settlement and, later, the unleashing of elk fecundity shaped and reshaped the park's landscapes in the relatively brief moment of a single century. Between the immediacy of people and elk and the snail's pace of geological forces, however, there is a third, time-related factor that has been critical to the making of Rocky Mountain's landscapes.

Fire is the force that has most influenced the vegetation of Rocky Mountain National Park, at least in the time frame that is measured by centuries rather than millennia. "Rocky Mountain forests," wrote Robert Peet, "are disturbance forests, with climax stands being less common than seral communities." He also observed that "for most of the Rocky Mountain landscape, fire has historically been the most important form of natural disturbance." Fire as a natural force in the making of the park's landscapes, however, has changed in recent times, primarily because of modern fire suppression. "The magnitude of the impact of modern fire suppression on forest communities throughout the Rockies," Peet concluded, "needs to be investigated."[1]

Investigations into how fire has affected Rocky Mountain National Park both before and after the era of modern fire suppression suggest that unbounded elk numbers are not the only threat to the park's ecological health and biological diversity. Human intervention in the frequency and intensity of fire has altered the natural history of the park and set the mountain enclave on a most unnatural course. Reaching an understanding of that course begins with an examination of how fire affected the Rocky Mountain ecosystem before settlers carved homesites out of its pristine environment and government agencies fireproofed its forests.

The evidence of fire in Rocky Mountain National Park "is reflected by the ubiquitous presence of charcoal beneath forests over the entire elevational gradient."[2] From ponderosa pine woodlands to spruce-fir forests, fire has shaped the shifting patterns of plant life in the valleys and mountains below tree line. Frederic Clements, who pioneered fire studies in the park, concluded at the turn of the century that "the study of burns in the park indicates an extraordinary succession of fires, encountered nowhere else in Colorado."[3] His studies, limited mostly to the eastern side of the park, revealed a mosaic of burned-over areas stretching from the base of Longs Peak to its tree line and extending from the southern terminus of the park to north of the city of Estes Park. Photographs taken between 1880 and 1920 confirm Clements's written observations, showing "enormous burns around the Park—in the Longs Peak, Glacier Basin, and Horseshoe Park areas, to name a few."[4]

The evidence of widespread fire in the park is less apparent today, erased in part by forest succession and the weathering effects of climate. But traces of burns from the late nineteenth and early twentieth centuries can still be found. At the edge of tree line, the skeletal remains of charred forests contrast sharply with the green spirals of slow-growing, immature spruce-fir forests. On slopes and in valley bottoms of the subalpine and montane zones of the park, there are extensive stands of young lodgepole pine, Douglas-fir, and ponderosa pine, forests born from flames and still decades, if not centuries, away from maturity. Fire is clearly critical to the natural history and ecology of Rocky Mountain National Park, a fact readily acknowledged by the park's fire management staff: "It cannot be disputed that the Park has a long association with free-burning fire and that its present forests have grown up in the wake of large fires. The evidence of past fire is widespread: Charcoal in the woods, burned stumps, long strips and broad patches of pioneer species like aspen, even-aged stands of lodgepole pine, and abundant burn scars along the subalpine region."[5]

Fire in the natural history of Rocky Mountain is both subtle and dramatic. According to Park Service figures, "on the average, the Park experiences four natural small fires a year; a large fire occurs at some location in the Park about once every 20 years . . . [and the] fire interval at a given location is 100 to 300 years."[6] In his study of fire management in the park, David Butts highlighted the subtlety of fire in the Rocky Mountain ecosystem. "The past fire frequency in this park," he observed, "has not been as intense as found in most of the western parks." His data showed an average of only two to three lightning fires a year in Rocky Mountain, a relatively small number compared to Yosemite, for example.[7]

Harry Clagg studied Rocky Mountain's fire ecology at the same time that Butts was examining fire management. Clagg's studies showed that the frequency of prehistoric fires in the park averaged fifteen years between burns that consumed more than ten acres.[8] His findings, however, did not address the behavior of fire across the park's elevational and vegetal gradients. In the park's ponderosa pine–Douglas-fir zone, for example, Kirk Rowdabaugh concluded that "recent evidence suggests a natural frequency of one fire every second year for the [entire] study area." He added that "studies of pre-historic records left by the trees themselves indicate the area's mean fire frequency is 84 years, some five times longer than the norm for this forest type."[9] In 1980 fire researchers revised Rowdabaugh's measurement of the average mean interval between fires in the ponderosa pine–Douglas-fir zone, arriving at a corrected estimate of forty-six years.[10]

Natural fire displays altogether different patterns in the lodgepole pine and the spruce-fir forests of Rocky Mountain National Park. Estimates of crown fire frequency vary from as little as fifty years in the lower-elevation, more xeric lodgepole pine communities to three hundred or more years in the cooler, moister spruce-fir forests.[11] More significantly, a comparison of studies of different vegetation zones shows a marked variation in the intensity and magnitude of fire in Rocky Mountain, pointing to the dramatic effect that fire has had in the natural history of the mountain enclave.

Fires in open ponderosa pine woodlands tend to be frequent surface fires fueled by grass. Ecologically, these fires help sustain a savannahlike landscape of uneven-aged trees—a landscape quilt of grassy patches intermingled with small stands and single individuals of ponderosa pine in a medley of age groups.[12] Midelevation fires in denser ponderosa pine and Douglas-fir stands are carried by both surface and tree crown fuels. These fires tend to be larger and more destructive, and thus they play a crucial role in maintaining seral aspen stands in the park's montane zone.[13] Finally, fires in the subalpine zone of lodgepole pine and spruce-fir are mostly "large crown fires [that] occur at long intervals but result in complete type conversion . . . that significantly alter[s] the mosaic of the area."[14] These fires have burned vast expanses of the park, helping to create the even-aged lodgepole pine stands that make up the majority of the park's forests and that endow the park's mountainous landscape with the striking quality of uniformity. In addition, these fires have opened up the landscape to transient grasslands and meadows and have helped maintain aspen groves at higher elevations. Despite the prevalence of intense crown fires at higher elevations, surface burns can occur near timberline and around high subalpine meadows. Such fires help create and sustain uneven-aged stands of lodgepole pine and help keep savannahlike spruce-fir forests open and accessible to wildlife.[15]

In the natural history of Rocky Mountain, fire has been a force for both preservation and destruction. In this sense it has had a dramatic and transforming effect on the landscapes of the park. Fire alone explains the shifting macro-patterns of plant communities (occurring in human, not geologic, time) over the park's quarter-million-acre expanse—and, for that matter, the persistence of plant communities that might otherwise have perished. Spruce-fir forests, consumed in dramatic conflagrations, have been replaced by tens of thousands of acres of successional lodgepole pine and aspen—forest types that, in centuries to come, will surrender to advancing spruce-fir. Fire has transformed steep mountain slopes covered with Douglas-fir into mixed aspen and ponderosa pine stands—stands that will be renewed to Douglas-fir with the passage of decades. The rolling hills and bottomlands of the park's winter range have been preserved in grassland and open pine woodlands by the grace of frequent but noncatastrophic fires.

AGE OF FIRE SUPPRESSION

Just as beaver and willow once rejuvenated the wetlands of Moraine Park, fire has perpetuated the vegetal mosaic of Rocky Mountain National Park. But the analogy between wetlands and forested slopes has another, more ominous side. Just as elk broke the cycle of water, willow, and beaver, people have disrupted the cycles of fire and revegetation, distorting natural processes and rhythms. Starting with the settlement of Estes Park in the 1860s, the historical pattern of frequent, low-intensity fires at low elevations and infrequent, high-intensity fires at high elevations changed dramatically.

From the mid-nineteenth century to about 1915, fire frequency increased in Rocky Mountain.[16] Fire scar studies by a number of ecologists point to an almost doubling in the frequency of fire during this period.[17] To explain the increase, researchers have suggested that human-caused fire—that is, fires lit by settlers to clear fields and by prospectors to clear entire mountainsides—supplemented the natural fire sources of lightning strikes and aboriginal fire practices.[18] The most affected part of Rocky Mountain was the montane zone, where the average mean fire return interval decreased to less than twenty years.[19] But Frederic Clements was reluctant to attribute all of the increase to human activity. "It is probably unjust," he wrote, "to attribute all the fires to man. During two summers' work nearly a dozen fires were noted which were due to lightning."[20]

During the 1920s Rocky Mountain was launched into the modern era of fire suppression, and the trend of increased fire frequency was abruptly reversed. Shortly after the area's designation as a national park, the Park Service followed the lead of the U.S. Forest Service and imposed a strict regime of fire control on all its parks. The symbol of protection for Rocky Mountain's valleys and mountains became Ranger Bob Flame, the Park Service's equivalent of Smokey Bear, who "fought for justice, captured outlaws, and faced death without fear."[21] Above all, Ranger Bob represented the last line of defense between conflagration and pristine forests. Posters carrying his message portrayed him as a heroic figure, confident and determined, standing in front of a V-shaped canyon of conifers, lakes, and waterfalls. Beyond the victory V and outside the boundaries of his protective and imposing presence stood the charred remains of a mountain forest.

Ostensibly fire suppression returned Rocky Mountain to natural patterns as fire frequencies declined dramatically and intervals between fires fell much closer to historical levels.[22] Skinner and Laven calculated that the ten-year mean fire frequencies for the Longs Peak region were 0.5 for the presettlement (natural) era, 1.3 for the settlement era, and 0.6 for the era of suppression.[23] Despite almost identical fire frequencies for the presettlement and suppression fire regimes, however, there was a vast difference between the fires of the past and the fires of the present. Human-caused fires—burns arising from human error, not from scientific calculation—were on the increase, and natural fires were on the wane.

David Butts reported that since 1930 three of every four fires in Rocky Mountain had been caused by humans.[24] Harry Clagg further observed that "control efforts by man have had little impact on decreasing the area burned during the last 70 years . . . [and] man-caused fires during that period have probably more than made up the small deficit in the area that might have been burned by lightning fires."[25] Similarly, Kirk Rowdabaugh concluded that "while organized fire control efforts may have reduced the acreage burned from lightning fires, the concurrent incidence of man-caused fires has acted to equalize the imbalance."[26] Fire had changed in the transition from the presettlement to the suppression eras—all three researchers acknowledged that. But to them, the change in the quality of fire—from lightning to human caused—was inconsequential compared to what they believed was a compensating factor: the apparent consistency in the quantity of fires in the two eras.

Butts, Clagg, and Rowdabaugh made wrong assumptions in their optimistic balancing act. Fire frequency had remained relatively constant, but the cumulative acreage burned had actually declined. In addition, nearly identical fire frequencies for two separate regimes of fire (lightning versus human caused) are not ecological equivalents. In the judgment of Rocky Mountain's fire management staff, "there is no reason to believe . . . that these two eras balance each other out."[27] Human-caused and lightning fires do not occur in the same areas and do not affect the same number of acres. Fires caused by humans occur most often where people congregate—in already human-impacted areas that are generally more accessible to fire crews and where fires can be more readily suppressed. Lightning fires—subject only to the seemingly random patterns of nature—affect both landscapes that have been touched and those untouched by people. Such fires have the potential of burning areas that are less accessible to fire crews, areas that can burn longer and more intensely.

During the past sixty years of active fire suppression, only three large blazes have burned in Rocky Mountain, and all of them were contained to approximately 1,000 acres or less.[28] The Ouzel fire, the most recent and the largest of the three, burned 1,050 acres in August and September of 1978. It ignited while Rocky Mountain National Park was operating under a new fire management plan—a 1972 plan that represented the park's first attempt to overturn and correct decades of fire suppression policy. Started by a lightning strike and confined to a few acres, the fire was left alone. After two weeks of smouldering, however, its dying embers were stirred by strong winds into a full-blown crown fire that threatened the nearby town of Allenspark. By the end of the Ouzel burn, the fire management plan was shelved and fire suppression once again became the official policy in Rocky Mountain.

For park fire staff, suppression during the twentieth century has meant "an exceptional period of fire exclusion" that argues "strenuously for fire in some form." Evidence is clear, they have claimed, that "with the advent of organized fire protection in the Park (roughly 1929), the frequency and size of fires has plummeted."[29] Fire may still be present in Rocky Mountain National Park, but it is no closer to replicating the natural processes of the past than are the unnaturally large herds of elk on the park's winter range. As Peet concluded in his survey of western forests, "the magnitude of the impact of modern fire suppression on forest communities throughout the Rockies needs to be investigated."[30] There is no better place to begin that investigation than in Rocky Mountain National Park, where naturally caused fire has all but disappeared.

At first glance, the reduction of natural, as opposed to human-caused, fire in Rocky Mountain is an anomaly. Fire suppression should have controlled only the magnitude of natural fires; it could not have lessened the number of lightning strikes or protected flammable timber from ignition. Fire suppression policy, no matter how strenuously enforced, could not have bent the forces of nature to human will. But according to Park Service data on fire in Rocky Mountain, natural ignitions have declined by nearly 75 percent since 1930.[31] Given that the frequency of fires during the presettlement and suppression eras is approximately the same, natural burns must have decreased by almost fourfold under Park Service management. Offsetting that decline, of course, has been an equivalent increase in human-caused fires.

The decline of natural fire in the park is not as mysterious as it may at first appear. Ignition has always taken one of two possible forms in Rocky Mountain. The first is high-elevation lightning strikes, "a phenomenon that characterizes the east side. Typically, lightning fires remain small, even during relatively dry seasons. Should foehn winds, like the chinook, rush over the Divide and push the flames into the tree canopy, a crown fire can result."[32] Fires of this nature are infrequent in Rocky Mountain, occurring at mean intervals ranging from up to two hundred years in lodgepole pine communities to well over three hundred years in spruce-fir communities.[33] Moreover, there is no way that suppression activities alone could affect the frequency of ignitions resulting from high-elevation lightning strikes. Although there is no evidence that normal patterns of summer convection storms have changed in recent times, it is possible that the enormous acreage converted to even-aged lodgepole pine forests in the wake of the fire-intense settlement era has dampened natural fire frequency. Because of their youthfulness, these forests have lacked fuels adequate to carry fire during much of the suppression period.[34] Yet stand immaturity is probably less important than the fact that high-elevation lodgepole pine is relatively burn resistant. To whatever extent the age of lodgepole pine forests has reduced fire frequency, its contribution must be considered minor in the historical context of lightning-ignited high-elevation burns. And because the frequency of high-elevation lightning strikes has probably remained constant over the years, reasons for the decline in natural fire in Rocky Mountain National Park must be sought elsewhere.

The origins of the second form of natural fire in Rocky Mountain lie at lower elevations, on the valley floors and the montane slopes where conditions are drier and surface fuels are more abundant. Frederic Clements observed in his study of lodgepole pine burns that "fires, regardless of the place and manner in which they started, would have developed and spread most rapidly in the lodgepole–Douglas fir zone . . . [but] undoubtedly many fires started in the upper grass land."[35] Once ignited, fires of this origin burned upslope, driven by local winds. Evidence of these upslope fires can be found in many of Rocky Mountain's low-elevation valleys, grassy bottoms that

> functioned, in effect, as a fuse to carry fire into the forests. In most years, fire would not burn in the damper, more protected woods; in other years, fire would continue up the slope. The lower elevation would recover fairly quickly, the upper slopes much more slowly—leaving vivid scars that could last well over a century. Thus, lower elevations showed a pattern of frequent low-intensity burning; the higher elevations, infrequent high-intensity crown fire.[36]

Direct lightning hits on valley bottoms and lower montane slopes undoubtedly accounted for some of the presettlement fires in Rocky Mountain. It is unlikely, however, that suppression activities have affected the frequency of low-elevation lightning strikes any more than they have influenced the frequency of high-elevation strikes. Nevertheless, it is possible that increased grazing pressure from elk has reduced valley fuels sufficiently that ignition by low-elevation lightning strikes is less likely. If this is true, a small part of the decline in natural fire frequency may be attributable to deterioration in winter-range conditions.

Another possible explanation for the decline in natural fires lies in the role played by Native Americans in the park's ecology. Although data are sparse, park naturalists believe that some of the upslope fires that historically burned in the area were caused by Indians who ignited grass to drive and capture big game.[37] Clearly the elimination of Native Americans from Estes Park by the beginning of the settlement era had an impact on the frequency of natural fires that has carried into the twentieth century. But it is unlikely that the lost contribution of Native Americans to natural fire frequency can account for more than a small fraction of the almost fourfold decline in natural fire that occurred in the passage from presettlement to the suppression era.

Ecologists who have studied Rocky Mountain's fire patterns have been perplexed by the abundant evidence of large fires in the park's history and the lack of evidence for fires today.[38] Fire suppression must be a factor, but explaining precisely how that factor has affected the frequency of natural fires has proven extremely difficult. So far, the best explanation is that low-elevation fires in Rocky Mountain were caused by more than direct lightning hits and aboriginal fire practices. Low-elevation ignitions outside the park—both lightning and Indian caused—may well have been the primary source of natural fires in Rocky Mountain.[39]

The evidence for this explanation is circumstantial, but persuasive nonetheless. Forest and fire ecologists from Colorado State University (CSU) were struck by a modern statistic: "In the surrounding Roosevelt National Forest the number of fire ignitions is five and one-half times greater than that for the study area [Rocky Mountain National Park]."[40] Their analysis also showed that 80 percent of the forty-eight fires that occurred in the park's montane zone between 1954 and 1973 had been caused by humans. Only ten of those fires had natural origins (that is, lightning). In other words, natural fires were occurring in Rocky Mountain National Park at a rate of one every two years—a mean interval dramatically below that of the surrounding national forest lands.

The CSU researchers determined that 80 percent of all fires reported in Rocky Mountain for the twenty-year period were a quarter-acre or less in size. Only one fire had burned more than ten acres, and that was a human-caused fire started accidentally in 1966. The researchers were shocked by "the apparent very low occurrence of natural fires in the area."[41] It simply did not make sense to them that the landscapes of Rocky Mountain, influenced by centuries of natural fire, should suddenly have become immune to anything but human-caused ignition. The answer to the anomaly, however, was not difficult to find. The solution was in the valleys and dry mountain slopes that encircled the relatively small mountain enclave.

Rocky Mountain National Park is not a complete ecosystem and it never has been. The natural fire processes that had shaped its landscapes for millennia were part of a larger pattern of fire that connected the area to the rest of the world.[42] Prior to the settlement era, lightning strikes (and occasionally Indian activity) ignited dry and highly flammable grasses, shrubs, and pine savannahs in the surrounding foothills and lower montane regions. The resulting flames would move up canyon bottoms and mountainsides toward higher and moister elevations that were relatively immune to the worst effects of direct lightning strikes. As a result, the forests and meadows that would become Rocky Mountain National Park burned at remarkably constant intervals, creating and renewing landscapes of immense vegetal diversity. Rocky Mountain's relative immunity to the natural and periodic ravages of upslope fires was the direct result of suppression efforts on adjacent U.S. Forest Service and privately owned lands. As those efforts took hold in the first decades of the twentieth century, the historical routes of fires were cut off. No longer could they move naturally from the relatively arid foothills outside the park into the wetter and cooler environment of Rocky Mountain's high montane and subalpine forests.

This hypothesis must still be rigorously tested, but it does explain better than any other theory the disappearance of natural fire from Rocky Mountain National Park—a situation maintained by Forest Service activities aimed at protecting the growing number of residences adjacent to Rocky Mountain's eastern boundary. Even if some better explanation is found, the fact remains that natural fire events and the ecological processes associated with them have changed substantially. Those processes must once again be put in motion if the park's status as biosphere reserve is to be protected and maintained. Rocky Mountain "is a 20th century forest" undergoing changes and disturbances that have severed its ecological ties with the past and set it on an uncertain and perilous course. As the National Park Service has described it,

> Since the establishment of the Park, that forest has matured in a fire vacuum, with minimal disturbances. One result is that the forest is now primed for fundamental transformations. Large expanses of aspen are now decadent. Even-aged stands of lodgepole have aged to the point that they are susceptible to infestation by the Rocky Mountain Pine Beetle. Spruce budworm has invaded mature spruce and Douglas fir. Some of this change would likely have been arrested and the forest rejuvenated had fire been present during the past 50 years.[43]

THE DECLINE OF DIVERSITY

Fire suppression in Rocky Mountain National Park is completing what elk began—the destruction of plant community and landscape diversity—and it is doing so on a much grander scale than congregations of elk on the park's winter range. The reduction in natural fires, the poorly understood product of the park's increasingly unnatural history, today eclipses overgrazing. Biological diversity as measured in the richness, mixture, and dispersion of species and communities—not in the absolute number of species—is endangered. At stake is nothing less than the survival of a unique slice of the

Rocky Mountain chain, a mountain enclave whose purpose is to provide "a standard against which the effect of man's impact on his environment can be measured," but whose emerging reality is something entirely different.

Rocky Mountain's declining aspen groves are the most conspicuous victims of fire suppression. They have paid the highest ecological price of any plant community for the decline in the frequency and intensity of natural fire. The visual evidence is compelling. Paired photographs of the eastern slope of Longs Peak taken in 1916 and 1986 reveal an unsettling change from diversity to monoculture. In the 1916 photo, aspen are conspicuous, interspersed as small clones among high-elevation forest stands and strikingly present as substantial groves extending from bottom slopes onto the valley floor. Seventy years later, except for a thin and often broken ribbon of aging aspen, the mountain slopes extending from valley bottom to tree line are clothed in near-continuous stands of dense lodgepole pine.[44] Although the paired photographs do not show the plant life growing on the floors of the time-separated forests, the changes on the ground are as dramatic as those visible in the forest canopies. The dense surface cover of grasses and wildflowers that flourished under the aspen is absent in the lodgepole pine forests. In its place are a few Rocky Mountain junipers and widely spaced grasses and flowering forbs. For the most part, the lodgepole pine forest floor is covered with dense needle duff, dead branches, and fallen trees.[45]

The Longs Peak landscape can be found throughout Rocky Mountain National Park, particularly on the terrain east of the Continental Divide. There the elk are inseparable from the landscape picture. They have played a major role in expediting the elimination of aspen on the park's winter range. But it is the absence of fire that has made aspen's downward spiral a one-way path to extinction rather than a natural interval in what was once a productive cycle.

Aspen in Rocky Mountain is primarily a successional species, dependent on fire for its renewal, maintenance, and perpetuation.[46] Before settlers arrived and before the advent of fire suppression, aspen groves thrived and perished in a natural cycle of renewal and rejuvenation—a cycle reminiscent of the natural history of beaver, willow, and water. Broad expanses of the park were dotted with aspen groves, and entire hillsides were at times cloaked in aspen's colorful and quaking canopy. Fir, spruce, and pine seedlings inevitably grew in aspen's cover, increasing in density over time and eventually spiraling above and shading the deciduous canopy. Deprived of light, aspen groves quickly became decadent; seedlings stopped growing; and the trees that were left aged, decayed, and toppled to the forest floor. Quickly filling the niche were stands of lodgepole pine, Douglas-fir, and spruce-fir, beneath which layers of fuels began to accumulate. Eventually a direct lightning hit or flames from an upslope fire ignited the fuels, consuming the crowns of conifers. Finally the circle was completed as aspen sprouts, stimulated by fire and cloned from the roots of a relic tree, recreated the groves and nurtured an explosion of understory grasses and wildflowers.

The suppression of natural fire disrupted the ecological rhythm of Rocky Mountain's aspen forests. The cyclical succession of aspen to fir, spruce, and pine and conifer to aspen has been severely and, in some cases, irretrievably interrupted. In the absence of fire, late seral conifer species may eventually dominate the park's landscapes at the expense of aspen stands that are not self-perpetuating.[47] The pending demise of aspen in the park has been known and understood for years by many of Rocky Mountain's researchers. Don Neff observed in 1955 that fire suppression had already significantly affected aspen regrowth and would, if continued, eliminate most of the park's stands within a few decades.[48] In 1983 Albert Parker and Kathleen Parker wrote that "continued aspen dominance on a site requires the perpetuation of a . . . fire regime."[49] Three years later, Frederic Nichols warned of the impending loss of aspen in Rocky Mountain: "Today wildfires are rapidly detected and actively suppressed. In the absence of stand destroying disturbances workers hypothesize that aspen is succeeding to other relatively shade tolerant species."[50]

Nichols's study is the most thorough account yet written on the ecology of aspen in Rocky Mountain. His findings leave no doubt that the park's aspen required fire for renewal, and that without fire, conifer succession would replace aspen, possibly forever. "Stand destroying fires and aspen's ability to flourish following fire," he concluded, "permitted aspen to survive in an area where continuing succession to shade tolerant conifers occurs. The presence of aspen in northcentral Colorado demonstrates the long-term effect of fire in this region. In the past, fire frequency was greater, and consequently aspen stand area was also probably greater. In the absence of stand destroying disturbances, aspen area will likely decrease."[51]

Missing from Nichols's scenario is mention of a loss from the park far more serious than the likely decrease of a deciduous species. Because of the dense, highly diverse grasses and wildflowers that thrive in its cover, aspen's demise entails a disproportionate attrition of wildlife habitat and food. Moreover, in the absence of natural fire to renew decadent aspen stands, biological diversity on Rocky Mountain's landscapes is fated to diminishment and eventual impoverishment. Scenes of grasses, shrubs, and wildflowers exploding in the wake of a forest-destroying disturbance, so evident in the aftermath of the 1978 Ouzel fire,[52] will become rare. Even in those few occurrences when fire creates the conditions for the growth of aspen stands, the likelihood of renewal and recovery will be compromised by the over-whelming presence of elk and their appetite for tender aspen shoots.

In the absence of natural fire, the monotonously even-aged stands of lodgepole pine that were created by settlement era burns and that now cloak much of the park's mountainous terrain and suffocate so much of its plant life will simply persist and stagnate. On more favorable sites, lodgepole pine stands will eventually give way to spruce-fir forests; but on the majority of the park's high-elevation landscapes, particularly the drier, windswept slopes and ridges, lodgepole pine will hold on, choking out the diverse plant life that might otherwise flourish.[53] Returning Rocky Mountain National Park to a regime of natural fire, of course, would not eliminate lodgepole pine, which is a fire-dependent species. "Under natural conditions," Clements observed, "the ascendancy of lodgepole will depend upon the frequence of fires."[54] Yet natural fires do more than perpetuate lodgepole pine forests; they also encourage landscape diversity.

Burns that occur randomly rather than those that are concentrated and intensified, as during the settlement era, would nurture patches of uneven-aged forests intermingled with successional meadows and transient aspen. Instead of the uniform forests that too easily enchant the park's visitors today, grassy openings and aspen clones mixed with young and old lodgepole pine stands would flourish and enhance the aesthetic and biological diversity of Rocky Mountain. The park would be less picture-perfect than it now appears, and it would lack the deceptive harmony and false beauty of uniform forests framed by granite peaks and azure blue sky. But ecologically, it would be healthy and vigorous.

In 1978 the Ouzel fire burned hundreds of acres of even-aged lodgepole pine over a two-month period. As Clements had predicted, lodgepole pine staged a recovery, but what emerged was anything but a monoculture.[55] In some areas the pine shared the burned slopes above Ouzel Lake with aspen. In other areas it grew in thickets. In some places it did not grow at all, apparently overwhelmed by the aggressive growth of meadows rich in grasses, wildflowers, and shrubbery. Eventually the entire area may once again be forested in uninterrupted lodgepole pine, but by then natural fire would be at work elsewhere, recreating comparable landscape diversity and vegetal complexity.

But natural fire has not been free to run its course, and the regime of fire suppression in Rocky Mountain has left its imprint on most of the park's lodgepole pine forests. For example, uneven-aged lodgepole pine stands—the result of low-intensity surface fires—are strikingly absent from the park's

Top photograph shows the high country lying above the far western end of Horseshoe Park and exemplifies the expansive stands of lodgepole pine that make up much of the park's forests. The bottom photograph shows a relatively mature stand of spruce-fir at the upper edge of Hidden Valley. Branches of limber pine are evident in the foreground. Photographs by author (June 1993).

A protruding finger of the 1978 Ouzel fire is evident in the center of the photograph. Prior to the burn, the scarred patch was a dense, depauperate stand of lodgepole pine similar to the forest that extends below and to the right in the background. As a result of the burn, however, the scarred patch now supports more plant species in greater profusion than before. Elsewhere in the burn area, species diversity is approaching the richness of the aspen-conifer hillside in the left foreground, itself the outcome of a much earlier fire. Photograph by author (June 1993).

abnormal, uniformly forested landscapes.[56] In all, patches of diversity—the outcomes of crucial disturbance processes and the vital signs of renewal—are conspicuously missing.[57] Nowhere is this more apparent than among paired photographs of Rocky Mountain's high slopes taken at the turn of the century and then again in 1986. The visual contrast is dramatic: landscape mosaics of varying stand structures, forest types, and open grasslands give way across time to uniform stretches of lodgepole pine.[58] Unfortunately the historical record of environmental damage does not stop at the boundaries of stagnating lodgepole pine forests. The legacy of fire suppression reaches into almost every plant community in Rocky Mountain.

Douglas-fir forests, naturally accustomed to periodic burns every forty to forty-five years, have especially felt the effects of fire suppression. By the late 1950s and early 1960s, these dense midelevation forests—freed from fire for only a half-century—had become overgrown with aging firs, stagnating seedlings, and densely clustered immature trees. By then conditions were ideal for catastrophic outbreaks of western spruce budworm. Starting in the 1960s and continuing through the 1980s, Rocky Mountain's Douglas-fir forests were hit by a series of spruce budworm epidemics. Today the evidence of those epidemics is widespread and visually dramatic. Almost every Douglas-fir stand in Rocky Mountain is dead or dying—the victim *ultimately* of fire suppression.[59] What should be dispersed landscapes of young and old as well as burned and dead Douglas-fir forests are now lifeless polygons of leafless trees encased in a uniform expanse of lodgepole pine.

What has happened to Douglas-fir is much more than susceptibility to the spruce budworm. Not only are such epidemics natural in the life history of Douglas-fir, they are also vital for sustaining critical ecological processes. Spruce budworm outbreaks pave the way for forest renewal by periodically ravaging older Douglas-fir stands, making the dead and dried timber ideally suited for ignition and consumption by fire. In the wake of fire, grasses and shrubs spread across the burned hillsides, providing abundant habitat for wildlife. Next ponderosa pine seedlings emerge from the grass-and-shrub canopy, initiating a process of succession and forest rejuvenation that leads ultimately to the reestablishment of mature Douglas-fir stands.[60] As a result, landscapes that otherwise would be dominated by stands of a single tree species support a continuously changing mosaic of vegetation. Like the legendary phoenix, highly diverse forest and range landscapes emerge in patches from the ashes of worm-infested trees.[61]

Fire suppression, however, has impeded the cycles of spruce budworm epidemics just as it has impacted the periodicity of fires. According to entomologists and forest ecologists from the U.S. Department of Agriculture and the Canadian Department of the Environment, "long-standing policies of fire control and harvesting techniques have had a great impact on forest succession and thus on susceptibility to budworm. . . . Fire control has caused a gradual shift toward climax vegetation—increasing the proportion of shade-tolerant species, which we now know are preferred by the budworm."[62] In Rocky Mountain, that shift is apparent in the uncommonly large expanses of Douglas-fir that have been decimated by spruce budworm. And although succession is taking place even in the absence of fire, the resulting landscapes are unnaturally homogenous. Instead of a patchwork quilt of early-, mid-, and late-successional Douglas-fir hillsides distributed randomly throughout the park, there is only a single dominant vegetal pattern: uniformily ravaged Douglas-fir stands.

At the very minimum, a resurgence of randomly occurring natural fires would break up the monotony of the landscape. It would temper the ecologi-

Skeletal remains of a Douglas-fir forest decimated by spruce budworm is prominent on the north-facing slopes along Wild Basin. The death and rebirth of Douglas-fir forests are natural phenomenon. Fire suppression, however, has given an unnatural twist to the cycle of perish and renewal by exaggerating the ecological impact of spruce budworm infestation. In addition, the sheer magnitude of dead and downed Douglas-fir contributes significantly to the park's accumulating fire-fuel load. Photograph by author (June 1993).

cal disruptions that decades of fire suppression have had on spruce budworm behavior and the structure of the park's Douglas-fir forests. But natural fires are not on the rebound in Rocky Mountain National Park. Rather, they remain relatively quiescent, and the consequences of that fact have become more apparent, and more unacceptable, with each passing year. Infected and ravaged stands that would and should have burned in the absence of man to make way for open spaces and youthful forests persist as nagging reminders of the underlying unnaturalness of Rocky Mountain National Park. Land-scapes bedecked in artificially fire-proofed climax Douglas-fir stands go year to year without reprieve from the ongoing assaults of western spruce budworm or hope of eventual cleansing by consuming flames. Worst of all, fuels build up daily, preparing for the moment when fire suppression will no longer be able to contain natural forces. Entire landscapes rather than selected stands will burn long and hot. Instead of creating diversity, fire will create confla-gration, and conflagration will result in more rather than less uniformity.

The effects of fire suppression have not stopped with Douglas-fir. They have also touched and distorted the park's ponderosa pine woodlands and its subalpine meadows. Grasses and wildflowers are slowly being edged out by trees because surface fires that historically sustained open pine savannahs are now less frequent and far less intense. The advance of ponderosa pine and the retreat of grasslands are dramatically recorded by time-series photographs taken of the park's valleys and lower montane slopes.[63] In addition, high-elevation wet and dry meadows are being invaded at their perimeters by advancing spruce-fir—for-ests whose ecological destiny, in the absence of fire, is to encase the park's subalpine in a continuous mantle of conifers.[64] In both cases, islands of diversity critical to wildlife and vital to the park's ecological health are being diminished.

Only the park's expansive subalpine spruce-fir forests appear to have escaped the consequences of fire suppression. But that fact merely reflects the relatively brief history of suppression compared to the enormous intervals of time that normally separate natural burns in the spruce-fir forest type.[65] Even in the relatively fireproof expanses of the spruce-fir subalpine, the decline of natural fire holds far-reaching implications for the future of Rocky Mountain National Park. Each year its forests, from timberline to valley bottom, come closer to disaster. In the opinion of park scientists and academic ecologists, the park stands at the brink of a major burn on the scale of the fires that scorched Yellowstone in 1988, but one whose consequences would be catastrophic for the wildlife that lives in Rocky Mountain and the human communities that surround it.[66]

After three-quarters of a century of fire suppression, the forests of Rocky Mountain are primed for fires that are anything but natural.[67] Decades' worth of dead and dying Douglas-fir that have accumulated in the absence of fire are the low-elevation tinderboxes that could ignite upslope fires of unprecedented magnitude. [68] All around McGregor Mountain and along portions of Bighorn Creek, downed Douglas-fir lie on one another in stacks as high as ten feet or more. [69] In addition, ponderosa pine stands that are now more like forests than woodlands because of their density hold the prospect of devastating crown fires. An abundance of small trees and seedlings in the understory may act as "fire ladders," carrying surface fires up into the crowns of three- and four-hundred-year-old pines. [70]

Even more threatening are the vast expanses of even-aged lodgepole pine. The stands are maturing, adding new fuels each year, and it is only a matter of time before those fuels are ignited by a direct lightning hit or an upslope fire. Once ignited, lodgepole pine forests will burn unimpeded, consuming vast areas of the park and threatening many of the towns and villages that surround Rocky Mountain. There will be none of the natural fire breaks that would have existed under a regime of unregulated fire. There will be no sharp variations in stand structures, no intermingling of meadows and forest groves, and no marked changes in diversity between plant communities to slow or stop advancing flames. Tens of thousands of acres of uninterrupted, highly flammable lodgepole pine forests will explode into an intense, uniform, and unmanageable fireball. [71]

Ignition of lodgepole pine forests on such a scale will undoubtedly carry dire consequences for Rocky Mountain's subalpine spruce-fir forests. Protected from burning for much of the twentieth century and resistant to natural ignition, spruce-fir stands will be defenseless against the catastrophic flames consuming downslope lodgepole pine. Given the right combinations of wind, temperature, and humidity, the fire will burn hotter and longer and will consume more acreage than any natural fire in the park's history. In the wake of the conflagration, the soils will be sterilized and seed needed for renewal will be destroyed. Generations of Americans and many generations of elk, deer, beaver, and ptarmigan will be denied the unheralded beauty and ecological richness of Rocky Mountain National Park.

Fire of such intensity may be tolerable in places like the Greater Yellowstone ecosystem, which includes Yellowstone National Park. There the acreage of wild lands is extensive enough to absorb conflagration without being completely consumed in the process. It is not tolerable in Rocky Mountain National Park, which is simply too small to contain a fire on the scale of the 1988 Yellowstone burns. Because of its size it lacks the margin of safety necessary to protect surrounding communities and at the same time prevent the wholesale consumption of the park in flames.

With luck the conflagration may never occur. But the mismanagement that has altered the natural history of Rocky Mountain and brought so much destruction to its land and life continues unabated. It is true that many of the changes in natural fire patterns are not the fault of park managers. Certainly they cannot be blamed for the suppression of upslope fires originating outside the park's boundaries or for the natural fire resistance of Rocky Mountain's even-aged lodgepole pine forests. Moreover, their reluctance to deviate from decades of fire suppression policy is understandable in many ways. Any fire policy other than complete suppression entails considerable risk that could engulf the park in flames, scorch surrounding communities, spark heated political controversy, and possibly end promising careers. The small size of Rocky Mountain and its correspondingly small margin of fire safety compounds the risk. Finally, adopting alternatives to fire suppression such as prescribed burns is easier said than done. Prescribed burns are not risk free; they are also costly to plan, implement, and control.

Risk, geography, and costs are the real-world constraints that have influenced the park's long-term commitment to fire suppression. They help to explain why administrators reversed Rocky Mountain's nascent 1972 fire plan in the wake of the 1978 Ouzel fire. Yet constraints, no matter how compelling they may seem, are never acceptable excuses for inaction; they are only reasons for caution. The Park Service's mandate is to preserve Rocky Mountain in a natural state,[72] much of which is dependent on fire-driven ecological processes. Whatever the constraints may be, administrators have a responsibility to restore fire to the park's ponderosa pine, Douglas-fir, lodgepole pine, and spruce-fir forests. They have little choice if they are to preserve and protect Rocky Mountain. That they have chosen otherwise for so long is a tragic indictment of park management. Rocky Mountain's caretakers must bear responsibility for the past they helped create. Constraints aside, they are clearly culpable for taking no corrective actions—especially at lower elevations—to alleviate the park's unnatural fire regime.

After three-quarters of a century of documenting the ecological disruptions caused by fire suppression, the National Park Service has failed to compensate for an ecological system that is no longer natural. It has failed to protect the biological diversity that is the park's lifeblood, a lapse in stewardship that has been lamented by research ecologists at Rocky Mountain.[73] The agency has watched Rocky Mountain National Park crumble into its component parts and lapse into decay; it has watched aspen fade from the landscape, Douglas-fir perish because of insects, ponderosa pine woodlands suffocate grasslands, meadows contract to nothing, and lodgepole pine forests march toward a fiery future. In the meantime, eliminating periodic burns in the park has accelerated the elk crisis by speeding the demise of aspen and diminishing the quantity and quality of grazing meadows.

A Colorado blue spruce streamside. Drawing by Shannon Lenz-Wall.

Rocky Mountain National Park is now on the verge of adopting a fire management plan that would end the era of fire suppression and bring the park into an era of prescribed burns (see Chapter 4). The plan aims to restore fire to its natural role in the Rocky Mountain ecosystem. But the plan is riddled with inconsistencies and deficiencies (many reflecting the high risks of letting fire burn freely), and there is no certainty that the park's administration will either sign off on it or be able to carry through on its recommendations if it is implemented. Regardless of what its future may be, the plan can neither hide nor disguise the long tradition of mismanagement that has endangered Rocky Mountain's landscapes and diminished the park's bounty of plants and wildlife.

SYMBOLS OF MISMANAGEMENT

Fire suppression and natural regulation of elk are the most conspicuous, but by no means the only, manifestations of Rocky Mountain's mismanagement. Colorado blue spruce is a case in point. It dramatically illustrates the toll being taken inside the park by bad policy and poor management. The namesake of Colorado and the pride of the state's citizens, the blue spruce grows in dense streamside stands, its blue-tinged crowns spiraling far above all other native conifers. It forms a unique wetland habitat in the Rocky Mountain region with a species richness disproportionate to the ground it covers.

In the Roosevelt National Forest, adjacent to the park, substantial communities of blue spruce can still be found.[74] But inside the park, the proclaimed sanctuary of Colorado's biological treasures, blue spruce stands are extremely rare.[75] Part of the problem is that Rocky Mountain National Park begins at the upper limits of Colorado blue spruce communities. As a result, the community type is naturally rare, occurring mostly on the eastern side of the park and then only at the lowest elevations.[76] The larger part of the problem, however, is that human activity, past and present, has damaged or destroyed the few blue spruce communities that once occupied the park's lowland canyons and streamside terraces.

Settlers were the first to disrupt and dismember the area's Colorado blue spruce communities. They cut the trees for construction materials and used the cleared benches along the mountain streams for homesites and livestock grazing. With the creation of Rocky Mountain National Park, logging, home construction, and cattle grazing stopped, but the assault on the blue spruce did not abate. Park Service campgrounds, picnic sites, trails, and recreation areas quickly displaced the few Colorado blue spruce stands that had managed to survive the era of settlement. An extensive stand of blue spruce at the western end of Horseshoe Park is now home to the large and heavily used Endovalley picnic area. And intensive recreational use has despoiled the few stands that can still be found in Wild Basin, at the western edge of Moraine Park, and along the lower reaches of Glacier Creek. Finally, the Aspenglen campground near the Fall River entrance has displaced the lingering remnants of a past Colorado blue spruce community.[77]

A rare community type—at least for Rocky Mountain National Park—is being systematically destroyed because its environment is too inviting to people. Streams and streamside vegetation that historically supported numerous plants and animals are now the official playgrounds, picnic areas, and hiking spots of park visitors. Adding irony to the bitter taste of biological loss, park administrators have made no effort to restore Colorado blue spruce communities depleted by past settlement. To date, park management of blue spruce has been limited to replacing camping with picnicking in Endovalley. As a result, streamsides and canyon bottoms that should support thriving blue spruce stands simply do not.[78] They are neglected, their recovery left to the vagaries of plant succession and the trampling footsteps of thousands of tourists. By every indication, the Park Service has remained loyal to past traditions and true to current management thinking.

Adherence to past traditions, of course, is understandable even if not fully excusable. Early in the park's history, when campgrounds and picnic areas were first being constructed and trails were being laid out, administrators were probably unaware of the rarity of blue spruce communities in Rocky Mountain—or, for that matter, of blue spruce's existence and importance. Only in recent years have park inventories identified blue spruce stands and have concerns for the protection of wetlands become a national environmental priority. Had Rocky Mountain's administrators taken the initiative, restoration and protection of the park's blue spruce communities could be under way at this moment.[79] But the initiative was not taken, and restoration and protection have not happened.

Today the Park Service channels its scarce resources into projects like restoring Big Meadows[80] or reclaiming fringe areas of the alpine tundra disturbed by human trampling.[81] But saving Big Meadows (a high-elevation wetland on the park's west side largely untouched by elk) while sacrificing the much larger wetlands of the park's winter range is nonsensical. And spending a small fortune to reclaim a minuscule slice of an otherwise healthy and intact alpine ecosystem is incomprehensible when measured against the plight of Colorado blue spruce. If any component of the park's biological diversity cries for attention, it is the ribbons of blue spruce stands that once graced a handful of streamside terraces and canyon bottoms on Rocky Mountain's eastern edge but that are now impoverished and endangered. Oddly enough, there may be more continuous blue spruce encircling the Kremlin in Moscow—a gift of the United States—than can now be found in the best of the park's campgrounds, river walks, and picnic areas.[82] Colorado blue spruce, like so many of the park's natural elements, is threatened and endangered in Rocky Mountain National Park—the victim of decades of official neglect and managerial disregard.

Sadly, Rocky Mountain's black bears share the fate of the park's blue spruce stands. The black bear population is currently estimated to be thirty animals, about half the number supported by equivalent habitat elsewhere and only half of what should be present in Rocky Mountain.[83] Part of the reason why there are so few bears may be Rocky Mountain's long history of fire suppression. The virtual elimination of natural fire has resulted in what Henry McCutchen has described as "an increase in mature stands of forest and a decrease in patches of earlier stages of plant succession." To McCutchen, the biologist who started Rocky Mountain's bear research program in 1985, "patches of earlier plant succession are important to bears," providing foods such as berries that simply cannot be found in forested areas.[84]

There is, however, a more compelling reason for Rocky Mountain's sparse bear population. Three-quarters of a century of bear control and avoidance conditioning by park authorities has created a creature so fearful of people that its usable habitat is limited to the most inaccessible regions of the park, only a small fraction of Rocky Mountain's 265,000 acres. Rocky Mountain's bears, McCutchen reported, "exhibit a model behavior that many other parks are striving for"—that is, an ingrained fear of humans and a resolute avoidance of human use areas. "Yet, this model behavior," he concluded, "exacts a cost from the bears although they are persisting in an area of high human use. In the park there is a network of human use travel corridors and centers of high human use with readily available high protein garbage. There are even human use areas in what we perceive as quality bear habitat (riparian areas, aspen stands), yet the bears avoid these areas and utilize the interstices within the human use web."[85]

A measure of the park's success in making bears fearful of humans and human-impacted environments is shown by the unusual behavior of a young female bear known simply as No. 3. The home range of No. 3 encompasses popular picnic and campground sites in Rocky Mountain, including the park's only ski area, Hidden Valley. When she was first captured and radio-collared in the summer of 1985, No. 3 weighed seventy-eight pounds. When she was reexamined the following winter in her den, she weighed only fifty-four pounds. McCutchen was surprised: "It is considered curious that this small bear's strategy for survival would be to risk starvation in the den and feed upon natural foods rather than forage upon readily available, high energy, human refuse within her home range.[86]

As curious as No. 3's behavior may have seemed to McCutchen, the bear was doing precisely what the Park Service wanted: staying away from people and avoiding the areas where they camped, hiked, skied, fished, and picnicked. By conditioning No. 3 to bypass such areas, however, the Park Service was constraining the young bear to some of the most ecologically marginal areas of her home range, thus also ensuring that the park's bear population would remain unnaturally low and that the health of bears like No. 3 would continue to be marginal at best. But that was apparently acceptable.

The Park Service had made the decision as early as 1915 that Rocky Mountain would be a home to tourists first and black bears second.[87] Treated as fugitives and hounded like trespassers, black bears did not even deserve the

Bear No. 3. Drawing by Shannon Lenz-Wall.

leftover garbage of human visitors. The best they warranted were the marginal and outlying park lands that people could neither use nor get to—the fragmented pieces of a home range rendered unnatural and obsolete by the caretakers of Rocky Mountain National Park. Bears had become strangers in their own land by 1990, facing many of the same pressures that had driven wolves and grizzly bears from the park. With the bears' habitat shrunken and their numbers abysmally low, McCutchen could not help but wonder if "the Park's black bear population [was] now at risk from similar pressures."[88]

Black bears are one small piece of the Rocky Mountain landscape. Their loss would certainly be regretted, but the picture-perfect image of the park would not be appreciably diminished. Yet black bears are like ptarmigan, beaver, willow, and blue spruce. All are indicators of the ecological health of Rocky Mountain National Park. Their collective demise in concert with the destruction of elk winter range, the disappearance of aspen, and the unnatural history of the park's forests makes a mockery of Rocky Mountain's intended purpose and renders meaningless the distinction of being a biosphere reserve.

Dedicated in 1976 as one of nature's last refuges from human intervention, Rocky Mountain National Park has evolved into a grotesque monument to human intervention, and it has done so under the caring stewardship of America's premier preservationist agency, the National Park Service. One cannot help but wonder how and why a mountain enclave of such infinite beauty could become in seventy-five brief years a park in such peril.

CHAPTER 4

Park in Peril

KILLING THE MESSENGER

By the winter of 1990–1991, Rocky Mountain's small staff of research ecologists was well aware of the environmental perils the park faced.[1] They had argued for prescribed burns in the park beginning in the early 1970s and had pointed out repeatedly to the superintendent the unnatural quality of Rocky Mountain's fire regime and the possibility of a major conflagration. So certain were they of the impending fire crisis that in 1989 they initiated a massive inventory and classification of the park's vegetation.[2] Such information about the plants and plant communities would provide a beginning point in restoring the park after the fire.

The park's research ecologists were also aware of the mounting biological crisis on Rocky Mountain's winter range, their awareness compromised only by their disagreement on its severity. In addition, they understood the political dangers that the crisis held for themselves and for the future of the park. David Stevens, head of the research staff, had two decades' worth of monitoring data that showed the depletion and degradation of the winter range. Henry McCutchen, the biologist in charge of the park's bear research program, had spent enough days in the field to know that weedy meadows, decadent aspen, and disappearing willows were not normal or natural. Richard Keigley, the park's botanist, had firsthand knowledge of the debilitating effects of management policy on major plant communities. He knew that it was bad science to reseed disturbed alpine roadsides with fast-growing exotic grasses—a project favored by the park's superintendent, but one that Keigley vigorously opposed. He knew with equal certainty the rarity of finding an intact Colorado blue spruce forest in the lowland canyons and streamside terraces of Rocky Mountain National Park.[3] Indeed, all three ecologists were acutely aware of the predicament of bear, beaver, and ptarmigan and the impact of elk on alpine and subalpine willow stands, wet meadows, and dry grasslands. But their efforts to point out these and other problems to the park's administration only worsened the already souring relationship that existed between them, a relationship finally unraveled by an unexpected reaction.[4]

In February 1991 James Thompson, superintendent of Rocky Mountain National Park, eliminated the park's science staff. He got rid of two of the three research ecology positions and effectively changed the third beyond recognition, ridding himself and the park of an embarrassing reminder of three-quarters of a century of failed policy and bad management. The reason for his action—at least in the opinions of Keigley, McCutchen, and Stevens—lay entangled in administrative quibblings largely incidental to the more pressing issues of elk and fire. Yet the practical effect of Thompson's decision was to strip Rocky Mountain of expertise and caring at a most critical juncture in the park's history, when its winter range and maturing forests faced ecological harm and havoc.

Keigley was reassigned to Yellowstone National Park, and McCutchen was sent to a National Park Service cooperative park studies unit at Northern Arizona University in Flagstaff. Stevens was kept at Rocky Mountain to deal with normal administrative duties, including the administrative tasks formerly handled by Keigley and McCutchen. As a result, he would no longer engage in biological research. His function would be to contract all scientific work to outside biologists and ecologists, consultants who would be less critical of park management and more amenable to close supervision.[5] Today Stevens is perceived as a threat to Rocky Mountain and treated as an outcast for heading a team of scientists that dared raise issues of great ecological import.[6]

A few other scientists who dared to speak up and criticize the park's policies received similar treatment. Richard Laven, professor of fire ecology at Colorado State University, believes that he was "black-hatted" because of his criticism of Rocky Mountain's fire management policy.[7] His experience and the fate of the park's research staff would seem to corroborate what Alston Chase found in Yellowstone National Park. The destruction of America's first national park, the evidence of which is given in stunning detail by Chase, was not the result of human error or the outcome of limited scientific knowledge but the direct consequence of park managers (mostly rangers) ignoring or overruling scientists in the management of the park.

Chase concluded that damage to the Yellowstone ecosystem occurred because "scientists became a separate caste" and "the Park Service [i.e., park rangers] went to work building a wall around science."[8] He observed that in building a wall around science and scientists, "rangers also built a wall around themselves. Insulated from the truth, they learned only what others wanted them to hear. Their management . . . became 'amateurish and political.' Indeed, according to a 1972 study of Park Service decision making by Daniel H. Henning of Eastern Montana College, 'wildlife rangers would not recommend anything concrete that the Superintendent might not support.'"[9]

Equally relevant to Rocky Mountain's predicament is Chase's claim that "in Yellowstone, rule by rangers and the decline of science were translated into practices that affected the future of wildlife. . . . Natural regulation, dressed in the trappings of a biological theory, gave policy the patina of academic respectability while real science was carefully prohibited."[10] Much the same thing appears to have happened in Rocky Mountain National Park. Good science was, and continues to be, subverted by and subordinated to a blind, inflexible devotion to the theory of natural regulation—or, more accurately, to the modified version of that theory. Like Yellowstone's northern ranges, Rocky Mountain's winter valleys have suffered the full gamut of abuses that come from too many elk and too little forage.

McCutchen is convinced that Yellowstone is an appropriate model for what has happened in Rocky Mountain. Certainly, science and research in Rocky Mountain have faced as many, if not more, obstacles.[11] In a paper on the history of science in the National Park system written just before his forced transfer from the park, McCutchen took sharp aim at "the revolving door succession of Service Directors and their appointed Science program leaders [which] has undoubtedly been a destabilizing influence [on science]." In addition, he attacked the perception by many park administrators that research scientists were "conducting studies not related to management needs."[12] All of these factors, he believed, had conspired to give science a low priority in the overall management scheme of the nation's parks. In Rocky Mountain and elsewhere, "policy [had resulted in] inefficient use and distribution of scientists and funding in regard to serious park problems. Concern has been expressed at the small size of the Service's science program in relation to the considerable information needs stemming from serious threats."[13]

Similarities between Yellowstone and Rocky Mountain, at least from McCutchen's perspective, go beyond the administrative dominance of park rangers and the impact of the "ranger mentality" on scientific research. Like Chase, McCutchen is extremely critical of the management theory of natural regulation. He sees it as a lame excuse for continuing do-nothing, custodial management at a time when aggressive management—such as elk population control—is necessary for the park's ecological well-being.[14] He strongly believes that natural regulation has failed in Yellowstone, and he knows it is failing in Rocky Mountain National Park. The reason is simple. Rocky Mountain is not a self-contained ecological unit where natural processes can function as they did before non-Indian settlement. Moreover, Rocky Mountain is not the pristine and natural environment that its managers would like it to be. McCutchen is probably right on both counts.

In 1915, when the Park Service took over management of the park, elk and beaver were rare, cattle were overgrazing the park's grasslands, and the patterns and rhythms of fire were anything but natural. Three-quarters of a century later, Rocky Mountain is even less natural. Elk have supplanted cattle as overgrazers; aspen are endangered; beavers and bears persist in numbers below their potential; wetlands are being extirpated on the park's winter range; and natural fire has been exiled from park landscapes that were born and nurtured by flames. Further, Rocky Mountain's quarter-million acres do not make up a complete ecosystem. Unlike the Alaskan megaparks or the Greater Yellowstone ecosystem, Rocky Mountain's land mass is too small to encompass the full range of physical and biological processes essential to its ecological health and soundness. Natural fires, like the wolves and grizzlies that once roamed Rocky Mountain and the elk that now consume its winter range, require more space to function naturally than the park can ever provide. Encircled by small villages and surrounded by summer residences, the park is an ecological relic in the midst of expanding urban sprawl.

THE LIMITS OF THE YELLOWSTONE METAPHOR

Alston Chase's Yellowstone is a convenient and seemingly appropriate model for explaining the plight of Rocky Mountain National Park. Science and scientists have certainly been ignored or distrusted at strategic times in Rocky Mountain's history. In 1991 they were summarily banished from the park, forced to give up the makeshift shed located in Rocky Mountain's maintenance quarters some 300 yards below the combined visitor center and office building that housed the park's superintendent and his fellow rangers. The elk and fire problems that troubled Stevens, McCutchen, and Keigley are strong proof that the promotion of the park as picture perfect is a cruel hoax, and that natural regulation and the park's claim to the title of biosphere reserve may be the cruelest hoax of all.

But there are limits to how far a metaphor can be stretched, and those limits are quickly exceeded in the case of Alston Chase's Yellowstone. Science and scientists have actually fared quite well over the course of Rocky Mountain's turbulent history. Each year dozens of researchers from universities all over the United States have come to the park to study everything from lichens to willows to geomorphic processes. That very few of them have dared comment on the park's deteriorating state speaks more to their professional ambitions—their desire to remain in the good graces of the park's management—than it does to the power of park rangers to silence criticism. Opportunity to speak out on the problems plaguing Rocky Mountain has never been denied to scientists. Silence has been their choice.

Moreover, Rocky Mountain's elk and fire problems did not arise because scientists were ignored or because park rangers chose to "play God" with Rocky Mountain's fragmented ecosystem. Even the theory of natural regulation cannot be blamed for what has happened. It would be a grievous error to assume, as Chase does, that simply substituting scientists for rangers in the park's administration could substantially improve Rocky Mountain's shaky status. Holmes Rolston, in a blistering critique of *Playing God in Yellowstone,* has countered that assumption. "Of all the options that Chase considers," Rolston wrote, "the one he seems to recommend would most deify resource managers and strong, scientific management."[15] Chase's option would make playing God in Yellowstone the full-time business of mortals transformed into deities.

All things considered, Rocky Mountain's history argues strongly against the genera of causes and prescriptions that Chase gave for Yellowstone's troubled environment. Among the factors affecting its natural history, the one that is most responsible for leading Rocky Mountain to the brink of environmental catastrophe has little to do with wrongheaded park rangers or slighted but well-intentioned scientists. Its remedy is most certainly not the deification of science or the elevation of scientists to positions of administrative authority. To understand how and why Rocky Mountain National Park has reached its present state, it is necessary to move beyond the value-laden parameters set by Alston Chase. We must view natural regulation anew.

THE GRAND EXPERIMENT

At its inception, Rocky Mountain National Park's version of natural regulation was not unreasonable. It was a vision of how nature should function, given the lofty goals of Rocky Mountain and the park's election to the select club of global biosphere reserves. Natural regulation was special and, in a basic sense, nearly divine. When Major Long's expedition arrived at the site of Rocky Mountain and observed large herds of elk, natural regulation was in force. Ute and Arapaho Indians supplemented the natural predation of wolves, and a network of migration routes leading to and from the park provided a constant safety valve for the prolific elk. "If anything in wildlife management can said to be divine," mused Rolston in his critique of Chase, "why not natural regulation—letting creation take its course?"[16]

Divinity, of course, was never the strong point of natural regulation—neither in 1820 when Captain Bell reported the shimmering blue strip on the prairie horizon, nor today when, by most measures, natural regulation has failed. But in 1968, when the experiment of natural regulation was beginning, other points argued in its favor—scientific considerations that seemingly compensated for the fragmented and unnatural features of the small mountain preserve. The managers and scientists who introduced natural regulation to Rocky Mountain understood the changes that had transformed the Estes valley since the arrival of white settlers. They knew that wolves, the natural predators of elk, were gone; that traditional elk wintering grounds and migration routes had been disrupted; that exotic plants had inundated the park because of past settlement; and that the human presence was on the upswing. They had read Ratcliff's 1941 study and had taken to heart its warning:

> The wintering area is restricted by private holdings both inside and outside the park boundaries. The village of Estes Park lies across a natural migration route to lower elevations. The country along the eastern boundary of the park is thickly occupied by ranches, numerous summer homes, and other forms of development, that keep the deer and elk crowded back on range that is at present very badly overgrazed.[17]

Despite these changes and transformations, park decision makers believed that enough remained of Rocky Mountain's pristine environment to constitute "an ecologically complete habitat." They believed that the park's winter range, "including some of the National Forest land, still possess[ed] the required complex of vegetation and physiographic sites" to sustain elk in a wild and natural state.[18] Essentially, they had an idea that could be tested in the tradition of scientific experimentation. Natural regulation would work if (1) elk numbers and forage conditions could stabilize without damage to either, and (2) hunting beyond the park's eastern boundaries could help regulate the size of elk herds just as migration routes had done in the past.[19]

Both of the conditions for the success of natural regulation were reasonable, and as hypotheses they were testable, given a well-designed regime of monitoring. In the minds of many, the park's elk control program in 1944 had started prematurely, ruining a first chance at testing natural regulation. Given just a little more time, elk numbers might have come into balance with the range's carrying capacity on their own. After all, Russell Grater had written that "no serious [elk] problem ... existed" when Rocky Mountain's elk control program began.[20] Further, it only made sense that habitat created by harvesting elk outside the park's boundaries would lure excess animals away from Rocky Mountain's beleaguered winter range.

Evidence, however, has not supported the 1968 experiment in natural regulation. Two and one-half decades of data collection and observation are reasonably conclusive: elk and forage have not reached a sustainable balance, and hunting beyond the park's boundaries has not reversed the destruction of Rocky Mountain's winter range. The severe winters that park scientists believed would help trim the overgrown herd have never materialized. Instead, elk numbers have kept on growing and vegetation conditions have continued to deteriorate. Nearly a quarter-century of experimentation has shown that natural regulation, in the absence of natural predators and historic migration routes, is not tenable in Rocky Mountain.

The evidence of the failure of natural regulation is overwhelming. Yet its failure is not what has transformed natural regulation into a force of ongoing destruction. The depletion of Rocky Mountain's winter range has come about because of a lapse in the scientific process, because what began as an experiment in 1968 became by 1990 a lesson in how best to avoid accountability for the health and welfare of Rocky Mountain National Park. Sadly, that lesson is deeply ingrained in the institutional fabric of Rocky Mountain, and it has been learned and practiced by rangers and researchers alike. Today administrators and ecologists share the blame for the damage that has diminished the beauty and diversity of the Estes valley. They are culpable because they failed to act.

A Matter of Accountability

Compelling evidence of the failure of natural regulation came early in the experiment designed to test its workability. Seven years after the program was initiated, when elk numbers were still below Hobbs's estimated winter range carrying capacity, Stevens reached a startling conclusion:

> With the residual effectiveness of hunting seasons outside the park and the public attitudes associated, it is becoming more important that in the future, public hunting cannot be depended on to control elk populations. It is also apparent that the park ecosystem has been severely disrupted as a result of human intrusion, both inside and outside, for many years. These changes, primarily in the balance of winter and

summer range, and the loss of historic migration routes, will probably need in time to be compensated for by artificial population control.[21]

Stevens hesitated to recommend immediate resumption of artificial population control because in 1975 there was a possibility that wolves would be reintroduced into Rocky Mountain. He believed it was scientifically "appropriate to allow the population to build at present rates . . . [but] if the reintroduction does not appear to be materializing, then a reduction [of elk] by trapping and transplanting *should be conducted within about two years.*"[22] Two years later, when it was clear that wolves would not be reintroduced, Stevens was silent. He did not repeat his recommendation for artificial control, and the park's administration did not act on his earlier counsel. The elk population continued to climb toward record levels.

By 1982 a combination of deteriorating winter range conditions and skyrocketing elk numbers led Stevens to conclude that action to curtail the expanding herd could no longer be postponed. He wrote,

> Data this year indicates that perhaps the [elk] population is exceeding what would be considered *natural* use levels. Although migrations are redeveloping, the human developments along the park boundary continue to build each year putting more pressure on the elk to remain in the park. . . . Plans for implementing alternative population control should be initiated. With the loss of hunting on the MacGregor Ranch, even with the present late January and February seasons, public hunting will not control the population numbers in the future.[23]

Again nothing happened. Rocky Mountain's superintendent ignored Stevens's second call for population control. He did this despite compelling evidence that argued for action. The experiment of natural regulation was a dismal failure, public hunting was not trimming the herd, and elk were not arriving at a balance with their winter environment. The superintendent's refusal to act directly violated the park's written policy on elk management: "If the present program is not successful in holding the elk population in check, and damage to the park ecosystem exceeds tolerance levels, resumption of control in the park will be necessary."[24] But for the next eight years, Stevens and his staff of researchers remained conspicuously silent in their written counsel, even though the annual ungulate condition and trend studies continued to reflect deteriorating conditions on the park's winter range. In 1988 Stevens briefly noted that "reproduction in the elk population continues to remain high with really no sign of a drop due to nutritional stress as might be expected."[25] Yet he gave no advice to enact population controls. A shroud of less-than-benign neglect enveloped Rocky Mountain in the mid-1980s, uniting managers and researchers in a conspiracy of silence that has continued to the present. Today elk numbers still mount, aspen and willows still suffer, and nothing has been done—except for the February 1991 banishment of Rocky Mountain's research staff.

A stampede away from accountability explains the inaction of both managers and scientists. In the case of Rocky Mountain's superintendents, for instance, controlling elk has always entailed political liability—a level of risk far greater than simply allowing the park's wild lands to suffer and decay.[26] A cavalcade of superintendents since 1968, six altogether, has made it easy for administrators to put off decisions. In office for only a few years, each superintendent has acted in his own self-interest, not in the interests of the park. Each has been faced with calculating the short-term political costs of trimming Rocky Mountain's elk herd, and each has apparently concluded that the price does not warrant the long-term environmental benefits—benefits that none of them could reap anyway, given the average tenure of seven years. A notable exception is the current superintendent, James Thompson, who has been in office for almost a decade. Since his arrival, he has made public statements alluding to the possibility that Rocky Mountain may have too many elk, but he has not backed up his words with action.[27] His retirement is near and his incentives are not substantially different from those of his predecessors. In all likelihood he will remain silent for the duration of his tenure, continuing to take the path of least resistance.

It is safe to say that all of Rocky Mountain's superintendents since 1968 have held to a course of inaction that entails the least controversy and the least risk to careers. Doing so has been particularly easy because it is elk that most visitors want to see when they come to Rocky Mountain.[28] Damaged winter range, if detectable at all to an untutored public, is more than compensated for by the sight of thousands of elk grazing the park's highly visible valley bottoms.[29] In their decision-making calculus, the park's superintendents have learned that the marginal cost of one more year of ecological decline is minuscule compared to the marginal benefits of more elk. Thousands of elk parading before the three million visitors who come to Rocky Mountain each year, and who vote for members of Congress who appropriate Rocky Mountain's budget, is well worth the loss of another aspen grove or the exile of another beaver.

In recent years park managers have found an even better excuse for not resuming artificial elk control. Continued severe overgrazing of park winter range has forced increasing numbers of elk to spend the winter season in the vacant lots and backyards of residents of the town of Estes Park. For most of the residents, the elk have become welcomed guests. No thought has been given to the fact that elk are there only because Rocky Mountain's winter range is in shambles. According to Catherine Berris, the author of a study on elk residence in Estes Park, "respondents were overwhelmingly positive about the presence of elk" and "elk reduction may be difficult to undertake due to public opinion."[30] Park managers like James Thompson understand that elk control adequate to protect Rocky Mountain's winter range would probably reduce, and might even decimate, the herd in downtown Estes Park—a politically unattractive prospect for administrators on the fast career track or close to retirement.

The burgeoning herd of elk in downtown Estes Park is an offshoot of the policy of natural regulation. It also represents a diminution of the wild and natural character of Rocky Mountain elk. "Since 1930," Lisa Zuraff wrote in a 1988 review of Park Service elk management policy, "it has been stated NPS policy to reduce the impact of man upon elk population."[31] Rocky Mountain's 1968 elk policy is even more specific: "It is the policy of the National Park Service . . . to maintain the natural abundance, *behavior,* diversity and *ecological integrity* of native animals as part of the ecosystem."[32] Despite these worthy intentions, the effect of natural regulation has been to create an elk herd that is neither wild in behavior nor natural in its ecological integrity. Elk have been increasingly driven to select the path of domestication. More mascot than wild, Rocky Mountain's wintering elk are becoming unintended victims of an experiment in natural regulation that long ago assumed unnatural proportions.

Escaping accountability and ignoring responsibility for what has happened to Rocky Mountain is not unique to park administrators. Rocky Mountain's science staff has also played that game and must share part of the blame. Researchers have been closest to the damage in the park and have recorded its minute details in annual reports dating back to 1968. To their credit, they stood up to the superintendent and paid the cost of doing so. But the cost was relatively minor: transfers to prestigious posts and supervisory authority over contracted park research. More significantly, none of the three researchers has ever made his findings and sentiments public. Stevens in particular has resisted making further recommendations for elk control—recommendations that he acknowledges must be acted upon if Rocky Mountain is ever to cope with its pressing environmental problems.[33]

Members of the science staff at Rocky Mountain have faced many of the same incentives that have compelled superintendents to flee accountability. Concerns for career and position within the National Park Service have consistently taken precedence in their plans and actions. This is not

More mascot than wild. Drawing by Shannon Lenz-Wall.

surprising. Like their bosses, researchers have had to weigh the costs and benefits of doing business on government time. After delivering warnings in 1976 and again in 1982, they received the clear message that nothing would be done, and that being team players, if only by virtue of their silence, was the best and least costly of the options. To protect themselves, they continued to collect data and record their findings, reporting annually to the superintendent as required. The incentive to do something more than their job, to blow the whistle on Rocky Mountain's winter range and bring the issue to public view, was simply not there. Their loyalty, whether by choice or necessity, lay more with the institution of the National Park Service than with the environment of Rocky Mountain National Park.

Stevens and his research staff also allowed themselves to be trapped by the circular logic of natural regulation: elk were natural, and therefore the destruction of winter range was a natural occurrence. The ambiguous concept of "naturalness" absolved Rocky Mountain's research ecologists of responsibility for elk destruction of aspen, wet meadows, and willow stands. In his interpretation of the winter range issue (one shared by many of his park colleagues), Stevens showed just how effortless and enticing the drift toward absolution could be. He made it clear that if the damage to the park's winter range had been caused by cattle, those cattle would have been removed immediately. Because the damage was done by elk, however, the standard for overgrazing had to be different. Under natural conditions, Stevens suggested, what appears to be overgrazing might actually be quite normal behavior.[34]

Such a rationale is specious. It demands that an objective person viewing a trampled meadow or a decaying aspen stand must see them as temples to nature on the one hand and as trashed environments on the other. But if that person did not know which animal had grazed the meadow or damaged the aspen, how could he or she arrive at the ecologically correct answer? Certainly the effect of defoliation is the same regardless of the animal involved. Moreover, it is a non sequitur to assert that because elk are natural, anything elk do or cause must also be natural.

The syllogism fails for two reasons. First, the elk of Rocky Mountain—at least the herd's population—*is not natural.* Elk numbers reflect the *unnatural* state of the park, a sliver of a larger ecosystem surrounded by encroaching urbanism. Like it or not, the park is a tiny island where natural predators no longer roam and where migration routes out of the park's winter range are blocked by highways, homes, towns, and cities. Simply put, Rocky Mountain is no Gates of the Arctic or, for that matter, no Denali or Greater Yellowstone. Certainly there was a time, long before boundaries made Rocky Mountain unnatural, when elk thrived on the park's summer and winter ranges. Overgrazing did not occur in those halcyon days—at least not the same way we attribute to domestic livestock. Predators and migration routes relieved excess population and encouraged a sustainable coevolution of grazing animals and plant communities. Today the world is much different. "Natural" elk in Rocky Mountain's highly urbanized setting are no more immune from overgrazing mountain ranges than are "unnatural" cattle in an otherwise pristine natural setting. The reason should be obvious. Overgrazing is neither a genetic trait nor a conditioned response that is in any way inherent in or specific to a particular species. Rather it is a function of the environmental factors that constrain, limit, and shape the behavior of a species. In this sense, domestic livestock and natural elk share an ecological fact of life.

Second, because the meaning of "natural" is ambiguous and because it is left undefined in park policy, its application in the management regime of natural regulation provides a convenient way to escape accountability. For instance, we can define the elk problem away by saying that disappearing willows, beavers, bears, ptarmigan, and aspen are part of the natural scheme of things. Assuredly, we have no historical reference to tell us what the area of Rocky Mountain National Park looked like before the advent of European settlement. Lacking such a reference point—what scientists term a biological control—we are left in a quandary: how do we determine what is and is not part of the natural scheme of things?

To begin with, neither scientists nor informed lay people appear to have difficulty identifying naturalness (or unnaturalness) in other landscapes where historical references are absent. For example, there are no photographs and written documents to tell us what the Roosevelt National Forest—the forest surrounding Rocky Mountain—looked like before loggers, miners, ranchers, and homesteaders arrived. Yet even in the absence of such biological controls, land managers and environmentalists rarely disagree on what constitutes severe livestock overgrazing. Denuded grasslands and trampled wetlands are viewed as natural settings only by the most recalcitrant defenders of public-land grazing. All others condemn such areas as unnatural.

If we apply the same reasoning to Rocky Mountain National Park, sound, defensible judgments on what is natural and what is unnatural are not only possible, they are absolutely necessary. To reiterate a crucial point, natural elk grazing in a human-impacted setting like Rocky Mountain can and does cause massive destruction of plant communities and vegetation. The evidence presented in Chapter 2 speaks for itself. Responsibility for that environmental destruction cannot be avoided by the circular argument that because elk are natural, the devastation they cause is natural and therefore acceptable. People are unavoidably part of the human-impacted environment we call Rocky Mountain National Park. It makes no difference whether the park's caretakers passively stand by or actively intervene in its ecology. Whichever strategy they select, their imprint is no less evident.

Playing God in Rocky Mountain National Park is simply another fact of ecological life. It involves unavoidable choices, which should, but do not always, entail responsibilities. Clearly, in an unnatural park like Rocky Mountain, *there is no correct population of elk*—at least none that can be justified in the name of natural forces. The final population of elk that finds refuge in the biosphere reserve will be by definition the product of human meddling and not the result of ecological processes long ago gone astray. Whether elk numbers continue to mount or not, people will be the cause. By the most elementary standards of right and wrong humans are the moral agents that ought to be answerable for disappearing willows, beavers, bears, ptarmigan, and aspen.

Despite all that has been said, there are still those who insist that because Rocky Mountain National Park is *supposed* to be natural, reliance on artificial population control of elk would subvert the park's high purpose.[35] Taken to its extreme, reasoning of this sort might even consider lifeless meadows and eroding hillsides normal and compatible with the park's purpose as long as elk participated in the transformation.[36] Such reasoning might even be applied to national forests, where naturalness is at a premium. Assuming that the current level of grazing in Rocky Mountain is producing natural conditions, and realizing that the park's policy of natural regulation has decimated elk populations in the surrounding Roosevelt National Forest,[37] we might want to increase livestock grazing in that forest by a factor of two or three. Once grasslands were adequately denuded, willows sufficiently razed, beaver populations appropriately trimmed, aspen stands largely eliminated, and wetlands devastated, we could phase out cattle to allow elk numbers to expand. The naturalness established by cattle could then be sustained by elk. Sadly, these are precisely the tactics and rationale (albeit grossly exaggerated in this latter example) that are used by Rocky Mountain's scientists and administrators to soften the harsh reality of too many elk on too little land.

The harvest of such tactics and rationale has been bountiful. In his ten-year report on deer and elk, Stevens explained away the loss of meadows, willows, and aspen in the park's winter range by claiming that "these successional changes are considered natural for an ecosystem with elk near the ecological carrying capacity."[38] He did not indicate just who considered such changes natural. He also failed to recognize that his explanation begged the original question of what is natural. These points, like the meaning of "natural," were left unaddressed in his report. Despite a record of speaking up on the problem of elk, Stevens and his colleagues at Rocky Mountain have nearly as often taken the opposite tack. They have, to the detriment of Rocky Mountain National Park, assumed a position of silence and complacency. They have exhibited what Frederic Wagner has termed "cognitive dissonance and tenacity bias,"[39] making natural regulation the rose-colored glasses through which data are filtered, reconfigured, and analyzed. More importantly, they have given themselves a convenient excuse for not making the elk issue a matter of public record. That silence, in turn, has made it much easier for Rocky Mountain's superintendent to rid himself and the park of scientists and to preserve the status quo of environmental decline on Rocky Mountain's winter range. Together, rangers and researchers have preserved a discredited idea and turned it into a hollow excuse for doing nothing.

The persistence of the idea of natural regulation in the face of over-whelmingly unfavorable evidence against it is reminiscent of David Bella's observation on the operations of the National Aeronautics and Space Administration (NASA) in the days leading up to the 1986 Challenger disaster. "Unfavorable information concerning risks," Bella wrote, "was filtered out right up to the time of launch. These systemic distortions resulted in misperceptions that, in turn, resulted in poor decisions."[40] Unpleasant information, information that did not support the status quo, simply did not make it to the top echelons of NASA. Scientists hesitated to express their concerns, making it easy for administrators to ignore fatal defects in the Challenger's rocket delivery system. Institutional failure and the death of Challenger's astronauts, Bella concluded, happened for reasons endemic to large institutions:

> In virtually every field of applied science, accountability is primarily administrative (that is, organizational) and "professional advancement" is nearly exclusively limited to "administrative advancement" in organizational systems. Those who advance in such a manner only rarely have either the interest or ability to defend their views in the open and disciplined communities that should characterize science. Efforts of administrators are directed toward sustaining the organizational process. . . . [As a result] if adequate steps are not taken, "scientific expertise" becomes a product not of scientific communities but of dominant organizational systems; applied science becomes the way organizational systems legitimate themselves. As one field person told me, "Science becomes the opiate of the people. It reassures people that all is well, and anyone who disagrees is not qualified."[41]

If Bella's conclusions are valid, they may shed further light on the widening gap between the way Rocky Mountain is managed and the reality of the park's winter range condition. We can better understand, if not accept, why administrators and scientists point to the nutritional health of elk as evidence that natural regulation is not the failure others have made it out to be. We can comprehend such reasoning *even though* Stevens's field data and the testimonies of his science staff conclusively demonstrate that the elks' nutritional health has been reached and maintained at the expense of the park's collage of plants and plant communities.[42] We can also understand, if not accept, why park officials have passed over the crisis of Rocky Mountain's winter range in favor of removing man-made drainage ditches from Big Meadows.[43] Recreating natural conditions in a small mountain meadow apparently takes precedence over protecting thousands of acres of wetlands, grasslands, and aspen groves. Symbolic yet relatively frivolous projects may not make good science or good sense, but they do make contemporary park management much more understandable. They tell us about institutional loyalties and incentives, clarifying in tragic detail the crisis of scientific accountability and responsibility in Rocky Mountain National Park.

But there is more. The history of fire management in Rocky Mountain resembles remarkably the tale and moral of elk on the winter range. It illustrates no less dramatically the failure of the park's mandated custodians to be accountable and responsible for its ecological health and biological well-being. Committed to a regime of fire suppression, park managers have done nothing for three-quarters of a century to return fire to its proper place in the Rocky Mountain ecosystem. As a result, unnatural patterns of forest structure (vast expanses of even-aged lodgepole pine), forest encroachment (movement of ponderosa pine and spruce-fir into grasslands and meadows), and forest decay (widespread death of aspen and Douglas-fir) now prevail over most of the park's landscape.

In 1972 the Park Service took the first step toward correcting the unnatural state of fire in Rocky Mountain National Park by adopting a let-burn management plan to reintroduce fire as a natural ecosystem process.[44] The opportunity to test the plan came on August 13, 1978, at a lightning-ignited burn near Ouzel Lake, south of Longs Peak in Wild Basin. Between August 13 and September 1, the fire burned slowly, consuming only a few acres of timber. Because of the fire's nonthreatening behavior, park personnel failed to monitor its progress, as required by the plan. On September 1, strong winds intensified the flames, threatening downslope population areas and forcing fire crews to initiate fire containment. By the time the fire stopped on September 16, largely because of a natural break in fuel loads, over a thousand acres had burned. Although the fire stayed within park boundaries, it alarmed area residents and jolted the park's administration. Subsequent investigation of the Ouzel fire revealed that the Park Service had failed to comply with its own fire management plan.[45]

The practical effect of the fire was to end the Park Service's fledgling effort to resurrect a natural fire regime in Rocky Mountain National Park. The superintendent wasted no time in canceling the 1972 fire management plan and restoring the ecologically untenable regime of fire suppression. In doing so he was allowing the park to continue its unnatural and hazardous course. The political dangers connected with continuing a let-burn policy were simply too real and imminent. One more error, one more miscalculation of wind speed or humidity, and his job and career might be lost. The dangers of conflagration from dying Douglas-fir and uninterrupted, even-aged lodgepole pine forests, as well as the crisis of diminishing plant community and landscape diversity, were more distant and, to the superintendent, less costly problems. In all likelihood, he would retire or be transferred from Rocky Mountain long before the problems of fire and diversity surfaced in public view. In the meantime, restoring fire suppression in Rocky Mountain was the quickest way to quell the firestorm of public debate.

Even if events had conspired to keep the park's let-burn policy in place, the plan's defects would have limited its effectiveness. It made no provision for prescribed burns, but without them there was no way the Park Service could compensate for Rocky Mountain's abnormally low frequency of natural ignition or the unnaturally uniform expanses of even-aged lodgepole pine. Moreover, the plan did not give park fire managers the necessary tools to deal with disappearing aspen, massive die-offs of Douglas-fir, and the relentless expansion of forests onto low-elevation grasslands and subalpine meadows. Properly designed and correctly used, prescribed fires could have broken up endless slopes of lodgepole pine and provided natural breaks against the possibility of conflagration. They could have been used to rejuvenate dying aspen, limit the devastation of western spruce budworm, and keep grasslands and meadows open and thriving.[46]

Since the Ouzel fire, the idea of reinstating natural fire in Rocky Mountain National Park has resurfaced from time to time, only to be beaten down by the political reality of events such as the Yellowstone fires of 1988. The Park Service is now considering a fire management plan based on a combined let-burn and prescribed-burn policy.[47] The intent of the plan is good. It aims at correcting the problems associated with abnormally low levels of natural fire, dead and dying aspen and Douglas-fir, thickening stands of ponderosa pine, and dangerously flammable expanses of even-aged lodgepole pine. But there is no guarantee that it will fare any better than the several draft plans prepared since 1985. The present plan, dated January 1992, is still under review, awaiting endorsement from the park's top echelon of managers.

Assuming that the plan will be approved and implemented in good faith, there are still serious problems with its provisions and underlying principles, problems that may doom it to follow in the footsteps of natural regulation. For example, the plan states that naturally ignited fires will be tightly controlled, not be allowed to burn unchecked. "It is important," the plan emphasizes, "that the public understand that *the NPS is not letting fires burn indiscriminately, but managing fires under strict, predetermined prescription criteria.*"[48] Given the small size of Rocky Mountain National Park, the bordering national forests, and the proximity of towns and residences, the plan is correct in placing limits on natural burns, particularly burns in lodgepole pine and spruce-fir, which have historically been large and intense.[49] But from the perspective of fire ecologists, those limits are too restrictive. Craig Axtell, Rocky Mountain's chief of resources management, believes that the plan compromises natural fire and that the constraints placed on natural fire will prevent it from resuming its normal function in the preservation and renewal of the park's landscapes.[50] The fact is that memories of the Ouzel and Yellowstone fires are still fresh in the minds of park managers. As long as the politics behind those memories prevail, natural fire will not be a major factor in Rocky Mountain's future. Like the forced removal of elk from the park's winter range, it will be privately discussed but never openly advocated. The environmental loss resulting from its suppression will remain just as free from the assignment of responsibility and accountability as the overgrazing of willows and aspen has been in the past.

The constraints that the Park Service has placed on natural fire make prescribed burning the centerpiece of the proposed fire management plan. It is the only tool in the Park Service's arsenal that can successfully avert the catastrophic burns predicted by fire and forest ecologists. It is also the best strategy to restore the ecology and natural functioning of aspen, Douglas-fir, and ponderosa pine.[51] However the remedy of prescribed fire is used, though, its application in the plan is guided by a basic and inviolable principle: prescribed burns are to be used only for the purpose of restoring fire to its natural role in the park.[52] Translated from policy to practice, this means that prescribed burns cannot be used for wildlife habitat improvement or restructuring forest stands to achieve stated landscape goals. Rather, prescribed fire must be dedicated to mimicking natural processes and to creating landscapes that are approximations of what might have existed naturally in the absence of non-Indian people.[53] Unfortunately, there is no universal consensus on the meaning of "natural," and in the fire management plan that meaning is left vague and largely undefined.

There are at least three criteria—three fundamental characteristics and preconditions—for defining and making sense of the term "natural" in the context of wild land fire management: criterion 1—living in or as if in a state of nature, untouched by the influence of civilization and society; criterion 2—free from artificiality, affectations, or constraint; and criterion 3—having a spontaneousness that suggests the natural world.[54] These criteria do not enjoy universal acceptance. Indeed, the very concept of "natural" has been challenged by fire ecologists who believe that defining it is futile and misleading. "I don't think there is such a thing as a truly natural landscape anywhere on earth today," Bruce Kilgore has written. "It seems to me that there needs to be a decision as to what kind of man-modified landscape we want in the future, followed by efforts to develop better ecologically sound measures to attain them. This is likely to be far more satisfactory in the long run than sterile arguments about what is 'natural.'"[55]

Nevertheless, Rocky Mountain's plan clearly gravitates toward a "natural" bias in the management of fire, just as elk management in the park has gravitated over time to an inflexible commitment to natural regulation. And just as there are pitfalls in the uncertain meaning of "natural regulation" of elk, so too are there dangers in the ambiguous meaning of "natural" when applied to prescribed burns. Prescribed burns are not natural either in design or effect. Such fires cannot, as the plan acknowledges, reinstate the historical frequency and intensity patterns of high- and low-elevation fire ignitions.[56] Prescribed burns are a break with the past and a clear divergence from the ways of nature. The reasons for this are clear.

Natural fires that individually consume tens of thousands of acres of timber are undesirable in a park whose entire area is not much larger than that. A scorched biosphere reserve, even if the product of nature, is socially and ecologically unacceptable. Moreover, prescribed fires are by nature limited. Their effectiveness, Laven has said, is not in their ability to imitate catastrophic, and often socially undesirable, natural burns but in their power to avoid conflagrations while achieving many of the ecological benefits of natural fire. As a consequence, prescribed fire in Rocky Mountain will, if properly implemented, create a forested landscape that is not strictly natural. Planned fires will reduce the probability of the large-scale, lightning-ignited crown fires common under natural conditions and will, as a consequence, modify the landscape patterns of vegetation in the park.[57] More diversity will reign in valleys and on mountain slopes, the outcome of widely dispersed but highly controlled burns. Patches of successional vegetation will enhance the park's life, possibly on an "unnatural" scale, and will offer effective breaks against potential conflagrations. These outcomes, however, are at odds with the plan's presumption of and bias toward "naturalness."

The needs and demands of good science are also at odds with the plan's presumptions and biases. Allegiance to the ambiguous concept of "natural" undermines the experimental nature of prescribed burns. Little is known about prescribed fire in the context of the park's unique environment. We are, in Laven's words, "at the bottom of the learning curve" when it comes to using or predicting the results of artificial burns. As a consequence, the application of prescribed fire to Rocky Mountain must be treated as an experiment, as a series of testable hypotheses, and not as a cookbook exercise in which all is known in advance. This means that fire managers must have standards by which to measure and assess the success and failure of prescribed burns and by which to modify or change prescribed burning to meet the park's needs.

Concepts like "natural" and "natural process" do not provide useful standards for the purposes of good science. Specific objectives such as improving elk habitat in a meadow or rejuvenating certain aspen groves do provide acceptable and usable standards, but they are precluded by the plan's bias toward "naturalness." As a result, prescribed burning cannot be objectively measured for success or failure. Because of that, there is the danger that it may mutate into what natural regulation has become: a self-justifying management regime unaffected by what happens to the land. If that happens, prescribed fire will evolve into the same calming prescription that natural regulation has become—one that makes people feel good because it is "natural" but that in reality perpetuates the environmental damage of the past.

There is another disturbing feature of Rocky Mountain's proposed fire management plan. Because "natural" is left undefined (and may well be undefinable) the park's plan cannot fail. Free of any objective standard by which to gauge its performance, fire managers can declare a prescribed burn successful simply by insisting that it is natural or that it mimics natural processes. Similar logic has already been applied to elk on winter range, and if applied to fire the implications are likely to be just as far reaching. Rocky Mountain's managers will have yet another excuse for not being responsible for the health of the park and for not being held accountable for the condition of its landscapes. The park's custodians can evade making decisions that might reflect their own values and judgments. In essence, they can claim neutrality, begging the question of their responsibility and absolving themselves of future accountability. They can also escape the political consequences that often attend tough decisions by blaming the forces of nature. In the process, they will condemn Rocky Mountain National Park to another century of mismanagement—to winter ranges less rich in flora, to forested slopes dangerously uniform in composition, and to a community of animal life more deficient than ever before. The mountain enclave as biosphere reserve will become in the worst possible sense "a standard against which the effects of man's impact on his environment can be measured."

Three-quarters of a century of Park Service management has brought Rocky Mountain to the brink of ecological disaster. Fire and elk that helped shape the living contours of the land long before the arrival of European settlers have lost their ecological moorings. Elk grazing, part of the environmental process that sustained the park's historical wildness, is no longer natural. Today its excesses fragment the ecological relationships that joined the living parts of Rocky Mountain into a vibrant whole greater than its individual parts. And fire, the primal force of ecological renewal and biological diversification, is no longer free to scour the land of the old and prepare the soil for the new. Its loss has diminished the wonder of Rocky Mountain and impoverished the complexity of its land and life. Although the first process, elk grazing, has exceeded its natural limits and the second, fire, has been constrained, the thread linking both is ecological imbalance. Disturbance, so vital to the life force of Rocky Mountain National Park, no longer sustains a healthy landscape. Too many elk and too little fire slowly devour, like a cancer, the living essence of the biosphere reserve.

FROM GOD TO GOOD NEIGHBOR

The unnatural history of Rocky Mountain National Park is not the by-product of "ranger mentality" or the policy-driven outcome of relegating scientists to second-class status in the Park Service administration, and it is certainly not the result of an environmental "theology"—what Alston Chase terms "the cosmology of deep ecologists"—corrupting management and science. Unlike Yellowstone, Rocky Mountain National Park has never been a focal point of environmental concern or a symbol around which national environmental groups have rallied. Because Rocky Mountain is free of the symbolic trappings that both distinguish and obscure more famous parks, understanding its environmental trials and ecological tribulations is that much easier. What has happened in Rocky Mountain is simply the consequence of institutional flight from responsibility and the accountability vacuum that has formed in its wake.

A crisis of accountability is striking at the heart of Rocky Mountain National Park. The form of that crisis can be seen in decadent aspen, disease-infested fir, abandoned beaver lodges, and dying willows. But those are merely the manifestations of the deeper problem. There is nothing intrinsically right or wrong about an overgrazed winter range or an adjacent mountain slope with fewer than usual aspen, fir, beavers, and willows. What makes landscapes right or wrong are the standards—the ethical guidelines—that humans apply in evaluating them. Standards of "naturalness" are as good as any, but they fail us by lacking definition. Scientific standards are equally ambivalent and subjective. There is nothing inscribed in the meadows of Rocky Mountain that proclaims that elk shall or shall not overgraze. Only our individual ethics can inform us whether overgrazing should or should not occur, or whether it is good or bad. If we choose to believe, as Aldo Leopold so eloquently did, that "a thing is right when it tends to preserve the integrity, stability, and beauty of the biotic community,"[58] then we do so because we want to, not because we must. In the final analysis, standards are no better than the people who envision them and apply them to the land.

The problem of standards—or more accurately, the problem of those who conceive and enforce them—is the contradiction that exists between people's perception that standards are objective and the reality that they are value laden. The managers and scientists in charge of Rocky Mountain National Park have tried to dress the value laden idea of "natural" and "naturalness" in the respectable garb of scientific objectivity. But by making natural regulation and prescribed "natural" fires icons of absolute truth, they have denied the human frailties upon which those ideas are built. Moreover, they have sought, albeit unsuccessfully, to make the standards and measures for managing the park unassailable by facts and immune to data. All of these factors have conspired to make environmental destruction in Rocky Mountain National Park inevitable.

Ironically, Alston Chase's advocacy of science leads to the same end point, but along a much different path. Chase has demanded that science and scientists set the standards by which national park landscapes are fashioned and managed. Science, he believes, liberates park management from the theology of "naturalness" and subjects human decision making to the absolute truths of physics and biology. But Chase has forgotten that physicists and biologists cannot tell us how a landscape should look. They cannot dictate whether there should be more or less elk, willows, or ptarmigan. All they can tell us is what to expect if we choose more or less of any of them. The larger question of how a park's landscape should be shaped and preserved remains a matter of the heart, an expression of human value that molds the worldly standards of both "naturalness" and science.

When people forget that there is a causal relationship between standards and values, they are guilty of a fatal conceit. They suspend their better judgment and surrender their will to what appear to be greater, absolute truths. In Rocky Mountain, the support of park managers for natural regulation has not waned despite dramatic evidence of its ecological failure. The same can be expected of standards that might be sanctified in the name of science. In either case, the outcome is the same: people are freed of the responsibility for decision making and spared accountability for what they do. These are not normal or natural states. Yet they are the conditions that thrive in Rocky Mountain National Park—the outcomes of institutional arrangements and incentives that have disconnected managers and scientists from the welfare of the land and its life. Today the cues that orchestrate the vibrant ecology of Rocky Mountain—the cues that disappearing willows communicate to beavers or that dying aspen convey to shade-loving plants— are not the same cues that orchestrate the working world of superintendents and ecologists. The bonds that should unite people and their environment simply do not exist.

The actions of those who have had the greatest role in shaping Rocky Mountain have been channeled along narrow institutional lines. Their livelihood has never depended on the health of the park. Their careers have not been built or dismantled on the outcomes of management success or failure. Survival and advancement for park managers and scientists have meant bending to the political will of Congress and submitting to the demands of lobbyists. Under such conditions it is not surprising that the path of least resistance for rangers and researchers has been to forsake accountability by seeking standards that absolve them of responsibility. Any standard would have worked, even the standard of science.

Rocky Mountain National Park will never be freed from the tyranny of standards or the caprice of human values. As an isolated preserve in an expanding urban area, its future lies in the hands of people. Its landscapes will continue to be influenced by human values and acts. There is no choice. People, as Rolston wisely observed, are fated to play God with nature; whatever they do affects the natural world.[59] The only choice to be made is whether those who stand guard over the park will acknowledge their own presence in the park's fragmented ecosystem and be fully answerable for the actions they take in Rocky Mountain's name.

What counts is not that they shield winter range from elk or insulate mountain slopes from conflagration. After all, there is no immutable standard for what a healthy park should look like. Ecology cannot tell us if more elk and less willows, aspen, and beaver is right or wrong. It can only tell us the implications of more or less. Ecology is simply a scientific tool and a scientific outlook that enlightens us in matters of process and consequence. Humans and their ethics, not the learned disciplines they dream up, are the final arbiters of the value-laden questions of right and wrong.[60] As hard as it may be to accept, there is no final answer to the question of the proper balance of elk, willows, aspen, and beaver—at least not in the human-impacted world of Rocky Mountain National Park. All that can be asked, and all that really matters, is that if elk overgraze or if the park burns from boundary to boundary, managers and scientists acknowledge and accept what they have done and pay whatever price may be entailed. This will not guarantee the best management, but it will ensure management that is better and more amenable to change.

If Rocky Mountain is to be rescued from the current accountability vacuum, ways must be found to reconnect managers and scientists to the land and life of the park. The interests of park staff must shift from political considerations to those of preserving and protecting Rocky Mountain. An institutional environment must be created in which scientists will have incentives to speak up and managers will have good reasons to listen more carefully. Above all, the caretakers of Rocky Mountain must have reasons to care for the park's health as much as they care for their own careers.[61] This can happen if the park becomes their careers—if Rocky Mountain's future and theirs become one and the same, freed from the interventions of politics and subject only to the natural constraints of responsibility and accountability.

CHAPTER 5

Restoring the Crown Jewel

DEAD-END REFORMS

Rocky Mountain National Park and the dozens of other parks and monuments that make up the national park system have one feature in common. Beyond the panoramas of sweeping grasslands, pristine forests, and majestic mountains lies the reality of crisis. Reminders of that crisis are almost everywhere. They are on the front pages and covers and in the special editions of newspapers, magazines, and journals. They are analyzed and detailed in a myriad of special reports and books that multiply each year. Despite this outflow of concern, however, the problem persists. The crisis that is being brought to the public's attention and the reforms that are being urged for its resolution bear little relationship to the cancer that is devouring Rocky Mountain and the cure that might restore its ecosystem. The mountain enclave is under siege by diagnoses and prescriptions that are insensitive to its crisis of accountability and irrelevant to its long-term ecological interests.

A Race Against Time, the National Parks and Conservation Association's (NPCA's) report on the threats facing national parks, is a prime example of insensitivity and irrelevance.[1] Its twenty-five pages are crammed with wrong diagnoses and bad prescriptions for parks like Rocky Mountain. Decaying infrastructure, burgeoning development, bad concession policies, scarcity of Park Service rangers, and an overflow of visitors are portrayed as the prime menaces to the national park system. The solutions are characterized as simple and straightforward, requiring only the largesse of a beneficent Congress. More money to rebuild roads, maintain trails, develop "sensitive" land use plans, buy out concessionaires, hire more park rangers, and build mass transit systems will halt the impending crisis facing America's parks, the report asserts.

Despite the best of intentions, the NPCA's report misses the mark for Rocky Mountain in almost every diagnosis and prescription. For example, it recognizes that urban development around the park "is blocking wildlife migration routes," but it concludes that "urban development in Estes Park and on the east side of the park is chewing up the winter range used by herds of elk . . . and causing aesthetic degradation and reducing public access from the perimeter of the park."[2] Nothing could be further from the truth. Winter range is being chewed up by elk, not by development, and the aesthetic degradation brought by more businesses and residences is minor compared to the ecological degradation caused by decades of overgrazing.

To suggest that urban sprawl is responsible for many of the park's problems is no more informative than pointing out that old age is the number one cause of death among senior citizens. There is no question that urban sprawl has disrupted elk migration, unraveled the ecological workings of natural regulation, and forever altered the ecology of fire in the park. In particular, there is consensus that development along the park's boundaries has diminished the effective winter range of Rocky Mountain's resident elk herd. But a shrunken winter range is not what has caused the failure of the natural regulation of elk. At best, it has accelerated the final verdict on natural regulation. At worst, it has intensified natural regulation's dismal ecological record. Still, the General Accounting Office considers "detrimental activities or sources located outside of the parks, including aesthetic degradation from land development" as among the principal threats to the ecological health of the nation's parks.[3]

Rocky Mountain's rocky past argues vehemently against such tidy excuses, which take the path of least resistance and cast blame on the easiest, most popular targets. The fact of outside development and mounting urban sprawl does not and cannot absolve the National Park Service of responsibility for damages done under the management regimes of natural regulation and fire suppression. The obligation of the Park Service—something overlooked in *A Race Against Time*—is to manage Rocky Mountain despite the real-world constraints of tourism and urbanism. Curtailing development and expanding Rocky Mountain's boundaries may be desirable, but short of confiscating private property and forcing tens of thousands of residents and seasonal visitors to relocate, it is an unrealistic goal.[4] More than that, it is a convenient alibi for the park's custodians and a false pretext for pumping more money and authority into the National Park Service. Its shining achievement is that it further diffuses responsibility and dissipates accountability.

NPCA's report fails Rocky Mountain National Park in other ways, too. The park's roads do need repair and its trails do need maintenance, but repairing almost a hundred miles of highways and maintaining many more miles of trails will not heal the park's winter range or restore fire to its proper place in the ecosystem. Better roads and more trails would make the lives of visitors easier without materially advancing the welfare of the park's plants and wildlife. Similarly, doubling the number of park rangers would not compensate for the loss of beaver, bear, and ptarmigan or the forced exile of science and scientists from the park's staff. At best, more rangers would merely swell the ranks of naturalists whose job is to entertain visitors—or, as the case may be, expand the number of police whose duty is to snare violators of park rules. Their presence would not inject new life into overgrazed and anemic willows or repel attacks by spruce budworm on weakened and dying Douglas-fir. Finally, three million tourists a year are undoubtedly excessive for a park the size of Rocky Mountain, especially if the values of solitude and wildness are to be protected and enhanced. Yet the solutions offered by the NPCA report—enlargement of park boundaries, better distribution of park visitors, and more national parks to relieve overcrowding—would only improve the quality of the park experience for people. They would not improve the quality of life for overgrazed meadows and decadent and decaying aspen, and they would not limit the fecundity of elk or restore the natural place of fire.

Regardless of wrong diagnoses and bad prescriptions, the popular press has used the NPCA report to identify what is wrong with Rocky Mountain National Park. Prior to the announcement of the report, the July 21, 1991, *Rocky Mountain News* contained an entire section headed "Parks Under Siege," giving the impression that Rocky Mountain was no different from other national parks when it came to the dual threats of too many people and too little money.[5] A month later, the *News* announced the release of the NPCA report, suggesting that residential development on the edge of Rocky Mountain National Park was symptomatic of the "development and industry . . . ringing our national parks in an ever-tightening noose."[6] More recently, *The Denver Post* zeroed in on overcrowding in the nation's most popular parks, suggesting that places like Rocky Mountain would soon have no choice but "to turn away tourists." James Thompson, superintendent of the park, provided the *Post* with perspective on the park's burgeoning people problem: "There are certain portions of every park that have some physical limitations, like parking lots. We reached that point several years ago and dealt with it through a transportation system, but it's not the ultimate answer [to overcrowding]."[7]

Thompson was correct, although not in the sense he intended. Mass transit systems are not the ultimate answer, nor is overcrowding the major problem facing Rocky Mountain National Park. Indeed, none of the points made by the NPCA and promoted by the popular press does justice to the critical problems facing the park. At the very worst, overcrowding, bad roads, development, and too few staff are mere irritants compared to the degradation of winter range and the deterioration of the park's forests. Such irritants might be considered real problems because they influence visitors' park experiences. But in a more important sense they are simply manifestations of a greater, underlying crisis: the absence of a strong and vital link connecting the interests of administrators and scientists to the ecological and environmental interests of Rocky Mountain National Park.

The significance of the missing link between managers and the park is evident in the so-called problem of overcrowding. As the situation stands now, solutions to overcrowding are necessarily political in nature. They deal with allocating a scarce public good to a polity that has equal claims to Rocky Mountain's landscapes. Because administrators and scientists operate in a world where the concerns of Congress and the dealings of lobbyists affect their livelihoods more than do the park's health and well-being, they cannot opt for solutions that make the most ecological sense or that have the least economic and environmental costs. Rocky Mountain's custodians lack the control that would encourage them to act responsibly to solve the problem of overcrowding. They also lack the incentives that come with control—incentives that would otherwise link them to the interests of the park and make them far more accountable for its worsening congestion.

Clearly, much more than dollars and additional rangers is needed to rescue Rocky Mountain from environmental decline. For solutions to work, they must attack the crisis of accountability: they must go to the heart of the park's institutional problems. One approach is to strengthen the position and role of science and scientists in the running of America's parks. The National Research Council (NRC) has recommended to Congress that science in the national park system be granted a clear-cut legislative mandate. Ideally, the NRC has stated, "legislation should be enacted to establish the explicit authority, mission, and objectives of a national park science program . . . to eliminate once and for all any ambiguities in the scientific responsibilities of the Park Service."[8] Further, the NRC has suggested, an external advisory board should be established to "provide long-term guidance in planning, evaluating, and setting policy for the science program."[9] Such "sweeping and fundamental" institutional changes, the council predicted, would help to ensure "faster, less expensive resolution of common problems and provide greater protection of the world's natural and cultural resources."[10] Most importantly, reform on this scale would encourage Park Service scientists to "challenge conventional wisdom and current policies and practices—with the single objective of improving the quality of science and management in the national parks."[11]

A legislative mandate for science would seem at first glance to be the ideal solution to Rocky Mountain's ailing environment. After all, park science and scientists have been ignored and abused in recent years, often to the detriment of the park's winter range, wildlife, and forests. But simply putting science on an equal footing with the administration of park operations, the heart of the NRC's reform package, would not correct the crisis of accountability that threatens Rocky Mountain's ecology. It would leave intact the institutional incentives that have distorted park management and that have made park superintendents more attentive to the demands of politics and bureaucracy than the needs of the land and its diverse life.

Science and scientists under the NRC's reform initiative would be just as susceptible to political meddling, bureaucratic intrusions, and bad institutional incentives as they are under the current administration. Ecologists and biologists empowered by new legislation would have no more reason to stick their necks out for Rocky Mountain than they do today. The same concerns of career, economic security, and abeyance to the wishes of local congressional delegations and special interest groups would continue to constrain their freedom and compromise their science.

Changes more fundamental than elevating science in the Park Service hierarchy are needed to provide the kinds of solutions that might heal overgrazed winter range and return fire to the ecology of Rocky Mountain National Park. Whatever scenario of change is finally selected, it must look beyond the problems of the agency's fledgling science program to the more fundamental, broader institutional problems that plague the National Park Service as a whole. A reform that seems to fit this description and that may be relevant to Rocky Mountain is offered by Michael Frome in his recent book, *Regreening the National Parks.* Apart from describing many of the ailments and recommending many of the cures highlighted by the National Parks and Conservation Association, Frome suggests a more radical solution: a complete revamping of the National Park Service. This would require that the National Park Service be reestablished "as an independent bureau, distinctly separate from the Department of the Interior and free of that department's chronic propensity for partisan politics and resource exploitation. Give it authority to challenge other federal agencies, like the Bureau of Reclamation and Federal Highway Authority, when their activities affect the parks."[12]

Frome's scheme would certainly enhance the power of the National Park Service bureaucracy by removing it from the stifling influence of the Secretary of the Interior. It is not, however, a useful prescription for what ails Rocky Mountain National Park. A more powerful Park Service would still be subject to the politics of congressional appropriations and would still be at the mercy of special interest groups. Administrators and scientists at Rocky Mountain would be no closer to shifting their focus and their interests from the needs of a mammoth bureaucracy to the needs of a small mountain preserve. They would have no more reason to be responsible and accountable for the park's winter range and forests than they have already been over the past seventy-five years.

Lorraine Mintzmyer, former director of the Rocky Mountain region of the National Park Service, is a case in point. She wielded administrative power over such national parks as Rocky Mountain and Yellowstone for over a decade. She gained national notoriety for her support of the 1991 planning document, "Vision for the Future: A Framework for Coordination in the Greater Yellowstone Area." The document called for a new working relationship between the Park Service and the Forest Service and made natural regulation the keystone of management in the Greater Yellowstone ecosystem. Special interest groups, fearing the document's effect on ranching, logging, and recreation, pushed the right political buttons, and in a dramatic demotion, Mintzmyer was reassigned to the mid-Atlantic region. Shortly afterwards she resigned from the Park Service.

Mintzmyer's fate would seem to vindicate Frome's prescription for Park Service independence. After all, politics in the Department of the Interior prevented her from trying innovations in Yellowstone's management, and it was politics that ousted her from administrative power. However, long before she collided with special interests in Yellowstone, she had had a free hand in the management of Rocky Mountain National Park. Because of her status as regional director; her close working relationship with James Thompson, first as her deputy director and later as her choice for superintendent; and the proximity of her Denver office to Rocky Mountain, she had unusually strong ties to, interests in, and knowledge of the park's administration.

Mintzmyer's close links to the business side of Rocky Mountain National Park, however, did not translate into a concerted effort to protect the park or come to its defense as she would later defend Yellowstone. She took no action to help Rocky Mountain even though the evidence at hand pointed to an ecological disaster in the making. During her regional administration over the park she remained silent. She did not fight for Rocky Mountain's embattled winter range when she had the power to act. Nor did she intervene in support of the park's science staff when Superintendent Thompson made his administrative move against Stevens, McCutchen, and Keigley. Indeed, Thompson's ability to act as he did almost certainly required the foreknowledge and concurrence of Mintzmyer.[13]

Rocky Mountain's environmental slide under Mintzmyer's administration highlights what may be the most potentially serious defect in Frome's reform initiative. An enhanced and highly centralized Park Service bureaucracy could actually accelerate already deteriorating conditions. It might, to a greater degree than before, separate and insulate administrators and scientists from pressing resource problems by building walls between them and the land and life of Rocky Mountain. Isolated from responsibility and accountability by a fortress bureaucracy, the park's rangers and researchers would have few incentives to rethink the management scheme of natural regulation or to reconsider how best to use prescribed fire.

Other remedies have been offered to cure the ills of national parks. The Park Service could take Joseph Sax's recommendations and remake Rocky Mountain into a sanctuary more befitting wildness and preservation—a cathedral consecrated to nature's divinity and dedicated to recreation "without handrails." The agency could allow the preservationist views that stress "naturalness" to dominate the park's management decisions. National parks that are heavily visited, Sax urged, should not be written off "as irrevocably urbanized." Plans "for the reduction of development" should be pursued "even more forcefully," he suggested. Above all, management dedicated to preservationist views should show "willingness to entertain the suggestion that the parks are more valuable as artifacts of culture than as commodity resources; a willingness to try a new departure in the use of leisure more demanding than conventional recreation; a sympathetic ear tuned to the claim for self-paternalism."[14] But given Rocky Mountain's experience with natural management, there is no guarantee that doing more of the same would achieve anything other than a repetition of the past. Indeed, encouraging the park to coast along on its already perilous course of natural regulation and prescribed "natural" burns might only heighten the crisis of mismanagement by further absolving administrators of responsibility and insulating scientists from accountability.

Enabling scientists to play a greater role in the park's administration (as opposed to simply making them equal with administration, as recommended by the National Research Council) would be no less a dead-end solution than the quick fixes of more dollars, more bureaucracy, and more preservation. Regardless of who calls the shots in Rocky Mountain, the unfortunate truth is that protecting careers, projecting the correct public image, and propagating as large a budget as possible (to study anything but the problems at hand) are more important than willows, blue spruce, beaver, ptarmigan, and bear. It takes an unjustified leap of faith to assume, as Alston Chase does for Yellowstone, that Rocky Mountain's problems can be largely attributed to the wrong people in control or can be solved by replacing those people with scientists. Nothing in the unfolding drama of resource deterioration in Rocky Mountain National Park supports such a supposition. If anything, the consistency of human behavior suggests that scientists appointed as superintendents would act no differently than their ranger counterparts have acted in the past.

A different solution to the problems of science, scientists, and scientific management on federal lands is being offered by Secretary of the Interior Bruce Babbitt. He has announced the formation of the National Biological Survey, an agency equal in rank to the Park Service and other Interior Department resource management bureaus. The agency's mandate is to inventory the biological resources of federal lands and to engage in basic research that is necessary for the protection and conservation of land, water, and wildlife. With its creation, Babbitt hopes to shield science and scientists from the distortions and disincentives of political intervention and bureaucratic intransigence.

Babbitt is probably correct that an independent scientific bureau will be relatively freer to pursue and more successful in conducting quality biological research. The model of the U.S. Geological Survey strongly supports this possibility. However, the creation of the National Biological Survey will absorb the vast majority of Park Service research scientists, including Henry McCutchen and Richard Keigley. Their departure from Park Service ranks will do little to resolve the complex management problems facing national parks like Rocky Mountain. We can hope that the Biological Survey will scrutinize the elk and fire issues at Rocky Mountain and recommend actions to undo the management legacy of the past. However, there is no guarantee that park administrators will listen to those recommendations. The history of interagency rivalry in the Department of the Interior is well known, and even if the current secretary intervenes in favor of the Biological Survey, there is no certainty that future secretaries will do the same.

More to the point, even if scientific information is successfully transferred between Biological Survey scientists and Rocky Mountain's administrators, the nagging problems of accountability and responsibility will remain. Under Babbitt's plan, scientists will have less attachment to the land and wildlife of Rocky Mountain than they do now. Their science will undoubtedly be solid and objective, but their commitment to the park will be fleeting and impersonal. Likewise, administrators and park resource managers will continue to face the same political and bureaucratic obstacles that make responsible and caring management difficult if not impossible. Good science will not change their institutional environments, nor will it automatically rescue the park from its troubled ecological state. At best, better science will make us think we have achieved our goals. At worst, it will blind us to the fact that we have not.

Restoring Rocky Mountain National Park to some semblance of its former pristine state calls for substantive solutions to the essential problems that undermine its ecology. It is unacceptable to sustain the illusion of a picture-perfect park by wasting time and effort on misidentified problems and inappropriate solutions. The litany of reforms tendered by would-be reformers—fewer visitors, more park rangers, less development, greater bureaucratic power, fewer concessions, and more science and preservation—does not begin to touch the crisis that is rendering Rocky Mountain a shadow of what it once was. Even if immediate reforms could be implemented ensuring reduction of elk numbers and reintroduction of fire, nothing substantative would have changed in the park. The long-term prognosis would still be clouded by bad incentives, entangling and disruptive lines of authority, and the ever-present threat of political intrusions. Only reform that addresses the issues of accountability and responsibility can reverse Rocky Mountain's unnatural history and reinstate its stature as a global biosphere reserve. For that to happen, the interests of Rocky Mountain and the interests of its caretakers must be the same.

THE CONSERVATION TRUST

Reforming Rocky Mountain National Park is not a matter of ideology; it is a matter of practical necessity. It is also a matter of providing the people who control the park's wild lands with opportunities and incentives to care. As things stand now, the National Park Service—the laborious chain of command stretching from the office of supervisor to the office of director— and the perverse incentives emanating from the politics of Congress and special interest groups serve only to limit opportunities and dampen caring. The reforms advanced by the NPCA, the National Research Council, Michael Frome, Joseph Sax, Alston Chase, and Interior Secretary Bruce Babbitt offer little in the way of substantive change that might alleviate the chronic ecosystem malaise of Rocky Mountain National Park.

An ecologically sounder future for Rocky Mountain, at least one that offers more than a winter range feed lot for elk and a tinderbox of even-aged lodgepole pine, must be built on basic reform that challenges traditional institutions and policies and creates opportunities and incentives for caring about a healthy ecosystem. Reform taken to this degree responds to the needs of both the park and its managers. It strives to forge a link of commonality between people and the land, making the interests and livelihoods of the park's managers and animal and plant life indivisible, interdependent, and harmonious. It seeks ways to refocus the attention and loyalty of park employees from the institutional demands of a highly centralized, politicized bureaucracy to the daily ecological and environmental needs and requirements of the park.[15] It also gives hope that biological diversity may finally assume its proper place in the management scheme of the mountain enclave. At the very least, administrators and scientists will see that some willows, some aspen, some bears, and some ptarmigan are preferable to none at all. They will be more likely to understand that protecting biological diversity in Rocky Mountain, especially the richness of plant communities and the heterogeniety of the park's landscapes, is the surest path to ecological recovery.

Effective reform of Rocky Mountain's administration entails changing the way people respond to their duties. It means that responsibility and accountability for the park's welfare must be assigned, accepted, and acknowledged as the inescapable consequences of human action. It also means that control over Rocky Mountain's fate must be exclusively in the hands of its custodians, not compromised by layers of bureaucracy or political intrusions. Simply stated, workable reform means removing barriers between people and the park. It means making the reality of overgrazed winter range and conflagration-prone forests so vivid and potentially painful that excuses and coverups will no longer absolve managers of the consequences of their actions.

There are few models from which to draw ideas for developing reform on the scale proposed here. If our purpose is to describe the minutiae of reform, the fine details of how it would work, then the paucity of examples is a serious handicap. But if our ambition is to explore the essential elements of workable reform, the features that might characterize it, we are on safer ground. We can focus on the process rather than the structure of reform, allowing ourselves a degree of modesty and flexibility in our deliberations. We can savor and develop particular reforms without endorsing them as final solutions. Moreover, we can indulge in ideas and approaches that might otherwise clash with bureaucratic constraints and congressional policy making. This is not to suggest that the plight of Rocky Mountain is less than urgent or that policy speculation is an affordable luxury. Our purpose in entertaining innovative reform is to quicken the pace of resolution, to expedite effective and long-term solutions to Rocky Mountain's problems.

Fortunately, the intellectual landscape is not entirely barren of relevant ideas. One plan is particularily noteworthy. In 1981 John Baden and Richard Stroup presented a novel proposal for saving America's wilderness areas.[16]

They suggested that government turn over America's existing wilderness system to qualified environmental groups, which would be free to manage wilderness areas in ways and by values most consistent with their preservationist goals. Such radical reform, they concluded, would liberate wilderness management from the political and bureaucratic machinations that have preyed upon America's wild lands. Most of all, the plan would put responsibility and accountability directly into the hands of those who have the most to gain from caring for wilderness and the most to lose from abusing it. To a greater extent than ever before, the interests of wilderness would mesh with the interests of its managers.

Although not designed with national parks in mind, Baden and Stroup's approach is conceptually enticing and pertinent to innovative park policy. It offers a strategy of reform that is adaptable to the predicament of Rocky Mountain National Park. The strategy would provide the opportunities and incentives needed to hasten the recovery of the winter range and to restore fire to the park's aspen, Douglas-fir, and lodgepole pine communities. The interests of administrators and scientists would shift from national politics and bureaucracy to the immediate needs of the Rocky Mountain environment and would forge the vital link between people and the land. Of course, this is only one of many possible solutions, but it helps clarify the essential elements of good reform and points in the direction toward which effective reform must proceed.

Reform fashioned from such a solution could be structured in any number of ways. One possible scenario would entail removing Rocky Mountain from the national park system and designating it as an independent and irrevocable Conservation Trust. The Trust, established by Congress, would be dedicated to the singular goal of maintaining and preserving the mountain enclave as a living, evolving example of the montane-to-alpine ecosystem of the central Rocky Mountain chain. There would be no congressional directive for its management other than the conditions already set by its designation as a biosphere reserve. Those conditions would be the park's controlling and constant covenants. Creation of the Trust in turn would pave the way for the ecological restoration of Rocky Mountain National Park, made possible not because of a new mandate but because of a better institutional setting in which to pursue the old mandate. No longer would there be a distant, centralized bureaucracy to restrict opportunities and diminish incentives for caring. The intrusion of politics would be minimized as the role of the executive and legislative branches of government in Rocky Mountain's future ceased. The land would still be public, at least in the sense of America's nonprofit public corporations, but the park would be independent, self-contained, and self-sufficient.

The care, control, and operation of the Trust would be given in perpetuity to those people whose lives are most entwined with the welfare of the park and whose interests most closely coincide with the ecological needs of aspen, willows, ptarmigan, and beaver. Rocky Mountain would become the sanctuary Enos Mills hoped for: a preserve where nature follows its own course, where the human presence is ephemeral, and where management intervenes only to enhance natural processes disrupted by urban sprawl. The park would be held in trust for the American people by employees of Rocky Mountain, faculty representatives from Colorado's principal colleges, and concerned shareholders drawn from the general public.

Rocky Mountain's Conservation Trust would be headed by a board of directors selected initially from the ranks of park staff and from the full faculties of Colorado's two major state universities. Five of the board's members would be freely elected from the pool of park employees. The remaining four, two each from the University of Colorado and Colorado State University, would be elected by majority vote of the faculties from each institution. The powers and obligations of the Trust would be limited to the selection of the superintendent and the setting of land management goals and policies. Matters relating to the daily operations of the Trust, in regard to both personnel and land management, would be dealt with by the superintendent and the Trust's paid staff.

Funding for the Conservation Trust would come from several sources. An interest-free federal loan, equal to Rocky Mountain's last two operational annual budgets and repayable within five years, would be granted at the time of the Trust's founding. Supplementing the loan would be fees collected from public visitors and income from provision of auxiliary services.[17] Fees collected in Rocky Mountain National Park would stay in Rocky Mountain, making the Trust autonomous.

The board of directors would also be able to sell membership shares in the Trust (at a price determined by the board). Because the Trust would be tax exempt, dividends would be paid in participation rights. Shareholders, made up of caring local residents, more geographically distant citizens dedicated to Rocky Mountain's protection, and concerned environmental organizations, would have the right to select from among themselves four additional members of the Trust's board of directors. That would bring the board's membership to its maximum size of thirteen. Various enticements might be used to attract shareholders, including special membership services and specific use privileges within the confines of Rocky Mountain. Receipts earned in this manner would be essential to retiring the federal start-up loan by the end of the five-year period. Once the loan was repaid, Rocky Mountain would be financially independent, no longer beholden to Congress for funding or to special interest groups for political favors.

Compared to the institutional structure that currently governs Rocky Mountain National Park and the popular reforms aimed at resuscitating its failing environment, the Conservation Trust would offer many advantages. Decision making would be freed from the heavy-handed dealings of special interest groups, and administrators and scientists would be able to act without first bowing to the will of Congress and the dictates of the National Park Service. Managers would be free of the political and institutional intrusions that have distracted them from the business of caring for Rocky Mountain. Financially independent of Congress, their incentives would shift from preserving budgets and careers to saving a biosphere reserve and protecting species diversity. The Trust's administrators and scientists would find it easier and less costly to make and enforce critical ecological decisions that might make the difference between more or less aspen, willows, ptarmigan, and beaver.

Political considerations that have sustained the unnatural longevity of natural regulation would, for the most part, cease to exist. The Trust's superintendent would face incentives completely unlike those faced by her predecessors. The primary concern would be meeting the preservation goals of Rocky Mountain rather than the career requirements of the Park Service or the budgetary requirements of Congress. The superintendent would quickly learn that it no longer pays to ignore the long-term environmental interests of the park. In order to secure her position, she would tether her personal and professional interests to the healing of winter range and to the future welfare of the Trust. She would have no choice. Responsibility for Rocky Mountain's health and well-being, no longer an inconvenience to be avoided or postponed, would stop at the superintendent's desk. Accountability would be her burden as well as her incentive.

Scientists would be freer to act and would be in much greater demand. The responsible and accountable superintendent would need their advice more than ever before. Scientists in turn would have greater reason to speak their minds and to remain loyal to the process of science and experimentation. Like the Trust's administrators, they would have a personal stake in the success of Rocky Mountain. There would be no avenues of escape left for ecologists wishing to absolve themselves from the demands of responsibility and the burdens of accountability. They, like all of the Trust's employees, would have to contribute to Rocky Mountain's protection or face the consequences of failure—the loss of employment, career, and a cherished environment. They would have little choice but to acknowledge the failure of natural regulation and to seek more effective means to check fecund elk. The same incentives would encourage administrators and scientists to jettison the policy of fire suppression and adopt a regime of natural and prescribed fires based on solid facts and good science. Experimentation and flexibility would supplant resistance and rigidity in the application of fire to the unnatural forests cloaking Rocky Mountain's slopes. Aspen would be given a second chance, Douglas-fir would green again, and hillside vegetation would be fractured into patches of diversity.

Healing Rocky Mountain's forests and winter range would assuredly be hastened by the allure of membership in the Conservation Trust. Individuals and organizations wishing to influence Rocky Mountain's future would have a more desirable option than the costly politics of lobbying. They could funnel their resources directly into the Trust's future by being part of the decision-making process. Their shares would give them a legitimate role in protecting and preserving values that used to be difficult to advance and defend. Trust members would have to assume the costs of their mistakes and endure the pain of their failures, but they would also be able to fully savor the pleasures of success.

Critics of the Conservation Trust plan might object that public membership would expose the Trust to economic exploitation. Such a fear is unwarranted. Even if all four public members of the Trust's board of directors had exploitive intentions, achieving their ends would require acquiescence from the remaining nine members. For that to happen, academics and scientists would have to unite with economic developers in a very unlikely and inherently unstable alliance. Moreover, in a small park like Rocky Mountain where abundant private services and accommodations are within about an hour's drive from any point in the park, developers and concessionaires would be unlikely to seek disproportionate influence on Rocky Mountain's governing board. The public component of the board would most likely be made up of a broad cross section of environmentalists, concerned residents, loyal visitors, and business people. A membership of such diversity would not pose a threat to the ecological integrity of Rocky Mountain National Park. If anything, it would add balance to a governing board heavily weighted in favor of scientists and academics. Whatever its composition, the board would effectively insulate the Conservation Trust from the political forces that now compromise and distract the park's administration.

Rocky Mountain would assume a distinctively local flavor. Preservation of the park would remain, as always, a matter of national interest, but achieving that preservation would be the job of local interests—interests that *become* local by virtue of commitment to place rather than attachment to distant, impersonal bureaucracy. Local interests in turn would be anything but provincial or "special." The membership of the trust would be diverse and naturally cosmopolitan. Ideas that before were shunned or ignored would now stand a much better chance of being heard and even adopted. Moreover, the special interests that lobby Congress and influence federal agency appropriations would be unnecessary, indeed obsolete, in an administrative environment of independence and local interests. Finally, the national interest of preserving wild and scenic landscapes for future generations would be served admirably by a Trust dedicated to the local environmental interests of Rocky Mountain National Park.

In the aftermath of the Conservation Trust's establishment, Rocky Mountain would be altogether different from what it is today. The picture-perfect illusion would be supplanted by concrete signs of ecological health. The expression of those signs might assume any number of forms—numbers of beaver and bear, perhaps, or the vigor of willows and aspen. Rocky Mountain's landscape features would reflect the indeterminacy of nature and the infinite stewardship potential that responsible, caring people can offer their environment.[18] Man and nature would be joined in a mutually beneficial compact, one where people would have incentives to care for aspen, willows, blue spruce, and bear and where nature would have the health to sustain its immense, varied bounty. The caretakers of Rocky Mountain National Park would at long last have cause to recognize and understand the full impact of developments outside the park on the ecological processes occurring within it. They would have reason to act soundly in the defense of the biosphere reserve.

Reform and rejuvenation of Rocky Mountain's administration and environment are reachable on the scale envisioned as long as reformers keep sight of the essential feature of the Conservation Trust—the reconnection of people to their environment. The idea is not new. Aldo Leopold saw it as the keystone of a land ethic and the precondition for changing "the role of *Homo sapiens* from conqueror of the land-community to plain member and citizen of it."[19] In the case of Rocky Mountain, eliminating the layers of bureaucracy and political organization that separate caretakers from their charge would be the first step in reconnecting people to the land. The remaining steps would be taken as incentives made caring easier and more likely and as institutional changes made responsibility and accountability a permanent part of Rocky Mountain's ecology. Commitment would strengthen among the land's caretakers in proportion to their exercise of control and their acceptance of responsibility. A community and ethic to match Leopold's vision would emerge incrementally, giving Rocky Mountain a chance to live up to its potential as a biosphere reserve.

Rocky Mountain National Park is unquestionably a unique, irreplaceable wonder, a shimmering blue strip of hope on the prairie horizon whose continuing destruction is shameful and whose prospective loss is unimaginable. Whether the idea of the Conservation Trust is tried or not, reform can no longer wait. Changes are needed in an institution that has failed to enforce the duty of responsibility and the ethic of accountability among its employees. Most of all, changes are needed to ensure that good stewardship becomes the final objective and the ultimate reward of those who have the privilege and obligation of caring for one of America's premier parks.

Bringing about constructive change in the national park system means enacting far-reaching reform, seeking innovative ways to harness the vested interests of caring people to the restoration of America's neglected crown jewels. It means piercing the illusion and getting down to the business of dealing with the problems that most imperil preserves like Rocky Mountain. It also means using the tools of decentralization, local democracy, and property rights, and the processes of the free market when possible, to attain public ends that public institutions have failed to reach.[20] Above all, effective reform means erasing the hypocrisy and scandal that clouds the title of biosphere reserve and ending once and for all a most unnatural chapter in the history of Rocky Mountain National Park.

Epilogue

Writing critically about a place I care for deeply has not been easy. It has been hard to step aside and clinically examine the object of my passion. It has been even harder to spell out a diagnosis that I know to be true but that so contradicts my first impressions of health and vigor, of forest-clad mountains soaring higher than I knew mountains could soar and dew-covered meadows and crystal-clear streams sparkling in the first light of dawn. But emotions must come to terms with facts: a very unnatural history has brought rocky times to Rocky Mountain National Park. A place of beauty and solitude, a landscape that has graced north-central Colorado for millennia, approaches the twenty-first century with prospects of decline and signs of decay.

In October 1992 I wrote about those problems in a guest opinion editorial published in the *Rocky Mountain News*.[1] I summarized what I have discussed in great detail in the preceding chapters. The "op-ed" turned out to be a lightning rod. The National Park Service reacted in a matter of days. James Thompson, the superintendent of Rocky Mountain National Park, sent a lengthy letter of rebuttal to me, with copies forwarded to the University Press of Colorado and several of my colleagues, including a former employer.[2] That letter, one of the last written by Thompson before his December 31, 1992, retirement from the Park Service, is the reason for this epilogue. It gave me the luxury of looking at the predicament of Rocky Mountain anew. It allowed me to clarify and enhance my thoughts and to add a fresh perspective to what I had already written.

Thompson began his letter by acknowledging that the "biological vitality of the park is coming under significant pressure." He added, however, that my op-ed had "overlooked or failed to mention the most significant issues and inaccurately characterized others." In particular, he felt that I had overlooked the "bright spots" in the park. My article, he asserted, had made no reference to the park's efforts to restore federally listed threatened species like the greenback cutthroat trout and the peregrine falcon. I had also failed to mention that Rocky Mountain National Park contains 10,900 acres of wetlands, that twenty more acres of wetlands had just been acquired with the addition of Lily Lake, and that even more acres of willow carrs were being sought near Copeland Lake. Indeed, I had failed to understand that the park's wetland problems were largely attributable to the Park Service not owning all of the water rights to the Colorado River. In addition, I had not included in my editorial the fact that the Park Service had hired a land use specialist to help mitigate land use changes outside the park's boundaries or that it had added a staff scientist to study the effects of global climate change on Rocky Mountain. Worse yet, I had failed to acknowledge the July 9, 1992, approval of a Fire Management Plan for Rocky Mountain National Park and its successful implementation with a "prescribed natural fire" the following September. Finally, I had overlooked the fact that the park administration was engaged in numerous restoration projects, including a project in Moraine Park to restore natural drainage.

As I read Thompson's letter over and over again, seeking some hint that the Park Service had at least a glimmer of understanding of what was happening to its biosphere reserve, a profound sense of sadness and despair swept over me. There was no anger. Indeed, I was glad to know that at least somewhere on Rocky Mountain's troubled terrain a few bright spots could be found. But bright spots could not erase the anguish I felt. I recalled an encounter I had had with a public land rancher and a Forest Service employee a few years earlier. When the agency scientist and I looked at the grazing allotment, we saw deep-cutting gullies, overgrazed and dying grasses, and stream banks trampled by hundreds of cattle. The rancher saw it differently. The gullies were natural; they had been there ever since he could remember, and they would probably be there long after he was gone. The overgrazed and dying grasses were the result of a dry summer, and the trampled stream banks were nothing compared to the damage caused by picnickers and off-road vehicles. There was truth in what the rancher said, but there was even greater truth in what he failed to mention and in what our eyes could clearly see.

Much the same can be said of the Park Service letter. The more I studied it the more I realized that the truth lay mostly in what Thompson had left unsaid. It is good that two threatened species have been restored. It is not good that park administrators have closed their eyes for so long to the massive destruction of habitat by too many elk and too little fire. Tragically, the habitat that has been lost once supported thousands of species, not merely two. It is correct that the park contains 10,900 acres of wetlands. They are a vital part of the park's ecology. That is why it is so catastrophic that so many of those acres, particularly those east of the Continental Divide, have been ravaged by unnatural numbers of elk. Certainly adding a place like Lily Lake to the park's wetland inventory is a prudent move. But it is incorrect to think that twenty additional acres of wetlands, especially wetlands located on a major highway and regularly trampled by visitors, will bring relief to a biosphere reserve already besieged by three-quarters of a century of mismanagement. Likewise, the acquisition of a few acres of willow carrs near Copeland Lake can never compensate for the hundreds of acres of willow carrs lost in Moraine Park, Beaver Meadows, Horseshoe Park, and the Kawuneeche Valley.

It is also wrong to attribute the park's wetland problems to the lack of water rights in the Colorado River and the diversion of the river's waters to the populous Front Range. Like the Grand Ditch in Rocky Mountain that channels the Colorado's water eastward across the Continental Divide, the excuse serves only to divert attention from the hard issues facing the park. The headwaters of the Colorado River flow from the western side of the park, not from the eastern side, where wetland destruction is most severe and most serious. An attrition in elk numbers on winter range is far more crucial to the welfare of the park's wetlands than an accumulation of water rights. Similarly, the hiring of a land use specialist to deal with land use changes outside of the park is inconsequential in light of the refusal of Rocky Mountain's administrators to tackle the most serious problem caused by external land use changes: the disruption of the natural checks and balances that once regulated elk population.

The recent addition of a full-time global climate change researcher to Rocky Mountain's depleted science staff is a fashionable move. It puts the park in the front rank of cutting-edge ecological research. But the importance of the new position is overshadowed by the September 1992 departure of David Stevens from Rocky Mountain, brought on by pressure from the park's administration.[3] The science staff may be unchanged in number, but it has changed most fundamentally in mission. Henceforth the park's scientific resources will be channeled into studying the potential future impacts of global warming on the park's ecosystem. The twenty-two-year monitoring program for elk on the park's winter range will be shelved with Stevens's departure. No one will be left to oversee the plants and wildlife of Rocky Mountain National Park, to stand sentinel over its threatened wetlands and endangered diversity.[4] A readily solvable problem of immediate and urgent proportions will be abandoned for a problem that is hypothetical at best and unavoidable at worst.

The approval and implementation of the January 1992 proposed Fire Management Plan (Chapter 4) appears to be a bright spot on the park's horizon. It signals Park Service recognition that fire can no longer be ignored in the ecology of Rocky Mountain. Indeed, the embryonic plan had its first test in September 1992 (and, as of July 1, 1993, its only test) when park resource managers applied it to a lightning-ignited fire at the lower end of Forest Canyon near Windy Gulch. The quarter-acre fire was successfully managed under the guidelines established for prescribed natural burns. However, there is a quantum difference between restoring fire to a land parcel smaller than most single-family suburban lots and restoring fire to a landscape of 265,000 acres. Moreover, the most crucial part of the plan—the setting of prescribed planned burns—will not begin until spring 1994. Certainly a fire management plan is needed to undo the ecological harm of the past, and in this regard the Park Service deserves our support and best wishes. But we must not forget other aspects of the past. We must remember the lessons of the natural regulation of elk, and we must be mindful of the impacts on fire policy that attended the Ouzel fire of 1978 and the Yellowstone conflagration of 1988. Above all, we must keep in mind the potential pitfalls and acknowledged shortcomings that will attend the new plan. Failures must be met with responsible and decisive action—virtues sorely wanting in the past management of the park. Clearly Rocky Mountain can ill-afford additional decades of well-intended plans gone astray. Good intentions are admirable, but good results are what will finally rescue Rocky Mountain National Park from the terrible legacy of fire suppression.

Finally, how can members of Rocky Mountain's administration find comfort in restoring natural drainage to Moraine Park when for a half-century they have allowed an unnatural elk herd to decimate its vegetation, destroy its beaver population, and play havoc with its natural hydrology? Yet the events in Moraine Park are consistent with other happenings in Rocky Mountain National Park. Besides funneling staff and dollars into the study of global warming, the park's administration is now pouring money into the reclamation of disturbed alpine areas around the park's Alpine Visitor Center.[5] One of the most visible and heavily used spots in the park, the center is a prime candidate for a face-lifting. However, the urgency of reclaiming a few acres out of tens of thousands of acres of undisturbed alpine tundra is minor compared to the urgency attending the ecological plight of the park's sizeable winter range—or, for that matter, the park's beseiged, poorly represented communities of Colorado blue spruce. If appearance rather than ecological condition and function truly drives park policy, as I have argued, then cosmetic surgery does make more sense than surgical excision of a growing cancer. That may explain why Richard Keigley fell out of favor with Rocky Mountain's administration when he resisted demands that he expedite the reclamation of disturbed alpine roadsides by seeding fast-growing exotic grasses.[6] It certainly helps to explain his forced reassignment to Yellowstone National Park.

The power of appearances may also explain why Lorraine Mintzmyer has fared so well in the aftermath of her directorship over the Rocky Mountain region. Today she is looked upon as an environmental heroine for her defense of the Yellowstone "Vision for the Future" document and her principled resignation from the National Park Service. But her image may entail more charisma than substance. Like the picture-perfect world of Rocky Mountain National Park, there is both more and less to Lorraine Mintzmyer than meets the eye. Under her administration, a chilly atmosphere settled over the region's scientific community, thwarting open exchange and encouraging the elimination of nearly half the region's scientific staff.[7] Science and research positions in Zion, Capitol Reef, Wind Cave, and Rocky Mountain national parks and two positions in the cooperative park studies units at Utah State University and Colorado State University were eliminated. Moreover, it was under Mintzmyer's administration that Rocky Mountain's winter range took an ecological nose dive and the park's forests inched closer to stagnation and conflagration.

The experiences of Park Service employees like Keigley and Mintzmyer are only symbols of what ails Rocky Mountain today. The full measure of the park's plight is best summed up by what is conspicuously missing in Thompson's letter. In four pages of single-spaced text there is not one mention of elk. The closest allusion to elk is the admission that "the most critical [issues] facing the park . . . are the land use changes occurring outside the park *which impact park values*" (emphasis added). Thompson is right. Land use changes beyond the park's boundaries lie at the heart of Rocky Mountain's ailing ecology. Land use changes are the reasons natural regulation has failed and will continue to fail. An urban ring around the park constricts winter range, rules out the reintroduction of wolves, makes restoration of historical elk migration routes unlikely, and severely limits the effectiveness of hunting as a tool for regulating elk numbers. The same urban ring plays havoc with the natural ecology of fire, blocking historical fire routes at lower elevations and making catastrophic high-elevation fires socially and politically unacceptable. For these reasons, neither elk nor fire retain their naturalness or function ecologically as they once did.

Too many elk and too little fire are the bane of a park too endowed with natural beauty to escape notice and people too human to abstain from desiring that beauty. Reminders are everywhere. We see them in meadows stripped of willows and purged of beaver. We feel them in the diseased and dying forests of aspen and Douglas-fir. We sense them in the plight of bears, in the strangulation of mountainsides by lodgepole pine, and in an unsettling sameness of a simplifying landscape. These haunting images assail our senses and sensibilities from every corner of the park. Yet as tragic as they are, and as angry as we may rightfully be, we must keep our thinking clear. It is not that elk are bad, and therefore fewer of them are desired. It is not that fire is good, and thus more of it is needed. Rather, it is a question of balance. Excesses of one and deficiencies of the other are the *cause* and the *effect* of Rocky Mountain's ailing ecology. Ecological imbalance is the legacy of beauty and desire; it is the defining characteristic of Eden undone and naturalness lost.

Like many lovers of Rocky Mountain National Park, I would like to believe that elk could reach a balance with the land without human intervention or that fire could somehow become wild again on a landscape that still has the trappings of wildness. An almost universal consensus among scientists and land managers precludes the latter. For fire to once again become an integral part of the Rocky Mountain ecosystem, it will have to be unnatural; it will have to be tamed and channeled by the cunning of people rather than the spontaneity of nature. Elk, however, are a different matter. There is no agreement among scientists and land managers on what should or can be done. Indeed, decades of park management suggest that it is an issue best avoided and, when possible, best forgotten. This is precisely what has happened. As a result, the biological and ecological loss to Rocky Mountain National Park has been immeasurable, only hinted at by the fragmentary data collected by one scientist over a period of twenty-two years across a physical expanse of 265,000 acres.

There is no turning back the clock in Rocky Mountain. "Naturalness" and wildness in the park can and should be strived for with the balanced understanding that neither of the two can ever be fully realized. For that reason, it is futile to bemoan the park's diminutive size or blame all of the park's ills on development along its boundaries. Even if Congress could afford to buy up expensive recreation land lying adjacent to the park, it is unlikely that many of the acres would be surrendered voluntarily. Moreover, it is fiscally irresponsible and morally objectionable to consider dislocating thousands of people by the exercise of eminent domain at this late date. From the pragmatic standpoint of cost and benefits, it is certain that America has social, economic, and conservation priorities far greater than the needs of a small biosphere reserve in the Colorado Rockies. Also, just as there is value in protecting Rocky Mountain, so too is there value in protecting the rights of innocent people. Deciding which set of values would best serve society is neither the objective nor the desire of this book or the reform package it offers.

Extending the argument further, a final answer to Rocky Mountain's ecological plight is also beyond the bounds of this book. The flaws in natural regulation have been discussed, and the options that face the park as the elk herd expands have been graphically portrayed. Certainly by now the reader has sensed my biases. Overgrazing by elk can and does occur, and my aversion to trampled, denuded, and scat-covered landscapes is in no way mitigated by the knowledge that "natural" elk rather than "unnatural" cattle committed the travesty. Given the choice, and this is exactly what is at stake in Rocky Mountain National Park, I would select more diversity in plants and wildlife over more elk, and more fire over miles and miles of mature, unbroken forests of lodgepole pine. I cannot say with finality that my vision is superior to that of those who wish to continue natural regulation, but I can say this much. I am certain that the most cavalier defender of natural regulation, if given responsibility for Rocky Mountain's future, would be reluctant to push the idea as far as it has already been pushed knowing that he or she would be held answerable for damages and losses incurred.

The issues of elk overgrazing and fire deficiency on the landscapes of Rocky Mountain National Park will be debated for years to come. The final answer—assuming, of course, that there is one—might take any number of forms. More or less fire and elk may be mandated by park edict. But edicts are one-shot solutions with no assurance of success and no probability of setting precedent, and if they fail there is no guarantee that anyone can or will be held accountable or that future generations will be any wiser for the lesson. The solution I have offered in Chapter 5 is a different type of answer. In fact, it is less an answer than it is a process—a way of arriving at solutions that are more responsible and more ecologically sound. The Conservation Trust should be seen in this light, as a potentially superior institutional arrangement for reaching quality decisions and implementing those decisions effectively. As such, the Conservation Trust is not and cannot be a panacea. There will always be problems plaguing the valleys and mountains of Rocky Mountain. I can only hope that if a new institution is adopted to protect the park's many wonders, it will perform better than the institution now assigned the role.

With the goal of building a better institution in mind, the Conservation Trust should also be seen as a vehicle for facilitating and encouraging honest and open discourse. If nothing else, I will be satisfied if my idea of a Trust either nudges or shoves the debate on America's national parks off dead center. Experts and lay people have criticized the national park system in infinite numbers of ways, but they have almost always turned to the same solutions of spending more dollars, hiring more "policemen," and building a more powerful bureaucracy.

I believe that Rocky Mountain deserves much better. It deserves people who care, whose ethics recognize it as more than a depository of resources or a laboratory where nature can be tinkered with to prove or disprove ecological theories. It demands people who ascribe to a land ethic and who firmly believe, with Aldo Leopold, "A thing is right when it tends to preserve the integrity, stability, and beauty of the biotic community. It is wrong when it tends otherwise."[8] Men and women committed to a land ethic will have to judge natural regulation and fire suppression by higher and more demanding standards than ever before. Attracting and empowering such people will require more than good luck, it will require good institutions.

Until those institutions are established, the best that the friends of Rocky Mountain can do is open their minds and hearts to new ideas. The Conservation Trust may or may not be the solution. But if we envision it as a first step, it could be the beginning of an honest and productive exploration. It could move us toward more innovative and viable alternatives, options that some day might measure up to the majesty and splendor that is Rocky Mountain National Park.

Notes

PREFACE

1. Karl Hess, "Phyto-Edaphic Study of Habitat Types of the Arapaho-Roosevelt National Forest, Colorado," Ph.D. diss., Colorado State University, Fort Collins (1981); Karl Hess and Clinton H. Wasser, "The Habitat Types of Region II, U.S. Forest Service: A Synthesis," U.S. Forest Service, Rocky Mountain Forest and Range Experiment Station, Fort Collins (1982); and Karl Hess and Robert R. Alexander, "Forest Vegetation of the Arapaho and Roosevelt National Forests in Central Colorado: A Habitat Type Classification," U.S. Forest Service, Rocky Mountain Forest and Range Experiment Station Paper RM-266, Fort Collins (1986). I also completed a habitat type classification for White River National Forest, located just south and west of Arapaho National Forest. See Karl Hess and Clinton H. Wasser, "The Grassland, Shrubland, and Forestland Habitat Types of the White River–Arapaho National Forest," U.S. Forest Service, Rocky Mountain Forest and Range Experiment Station, Fort Collins (1982).

2. One product of that shift in focus was Karl Hess, *Visions Upon the Land: Man and Nature on the Western Range* (Washington, D.C.: Island Press, 1992).

3. The science staff viewed the inventory information I was to collect as a hedge against a looming threat. If Rocky Mountain were to be struck by a major fire—a prospect all too real to both Stevens and McCutchen—then my study would serve as a road map for the future. It would show what had been lost, and it would provide guidelines for interpretation, management, and restoration.

4. Karl Hess, "Final Report: Description and Evaluation of Cover Types in the Rocky Mountain National Park," Rocky Mountain National Park, Estes Park (1991). My involvement in the Rocky Mountain

study ended in the fall of 1991, after verification of a plant cover–type map for the park was completed.

CHAPTER 1: INTRODUCTION

1. Harlin M. Fuller and Leroy R. Hafen, *The Journal of Captain John R. Bell* (Glendale, Calif.: Arthur H. Clark Co., 1973), 142.

2. Ibid., 5.

3. C.W. Buchholtz, *Rocky Mountain National Park: A History* (Boulder: Colorado Associated University Press, 1983), 12.

4. Enos A. Mills, *The Rocky Mountain National Park* (Garden City, N.Y.: Doubleday, Page & Company, 1924), 3.

5. David R. Stevens, "The Deer and Elk of Rocky Mountain National Park: A Ten-Year Study," Rocky Mountain National Park, Estes Park (1980), 4.

6. Milton Estes, "The Memoirs of Estes Park," *Colorado Magazine* 16,4 (1939), 121–132.

7. Stevens, "The Deer and Elk of Rocky Mountain National Park," 5. Grizzly bears are mentioned in Buchholtz, *Rocky Mountain National Park*, and Joe Mills, *A Mountain Boyhood* (Lincoln: University of Nebraska Press, 1988). Park naturalists believe grizzlies became extinct in the area shortly after its designation as a national park in 1915.

8. Although the larger sawmills did not find long-term opportunities in Rocky Mountain, smaller mills were built and did have localized impacts. Two such mills severely affected the Mill Creek and Hidden Valley areas of the park.

9. E. Mills, *The Rocky Mountain National Park*, 19.

10. Ibid., 23.

11. Ibid., 19.

12. Buchholtz, *Rocky Mountain National Park*, 132.

13. Enos Mills's efforts on behalf of Rocky Mountain National Park, and U.S. Forest Service opposition to its designation as a national park, are noted in Buchholtz, *The Rocky Mountain National Park*, 88 and 104. The Forest Service claimed that the steep slopes of Rocky

Mountain were only good for livestock grazing.

14. U.S. Codes, 38 U.S. Statutes 798 (January 26, 1915).

15. Wilderness Act, U.S. Public Law 88-577, 78 U.S. Statutes (September 3, 1964).

16. See National Park Service, "Vegetation Cover Survey for Rocky Mountain National Park," Rocky Mountain National Park, Branch of Forestry, Estes Park (1935–1936); Kenneth F. Bierly, "Meadow and Fen Vegetation in Big Meadows," Rocky Mountain National Park, M.S. thesis, Colorado State University, Fort Collins (1972); Robert K. Peet, "Forest Vegetation of the East Slope of the Northern Colorado Front Range," Ph.D. diss., Cornell University, Ithaca, N.Y. (1975); and Karl Hess, "Final Report: Description and Evaluation of Cover Types in the Rocky Mountain National Park," Rocky Mountain National Park, Estes Park (1991).

17. Figures on 1991 annual visitation were provided by Rocky Mountain and Yellowstone national park staff.

18. Transcribed from the commemorative plaque located at Rocky Mountain National Park headquarters, Estes Park. Emphasis added.

19. See Betty E. Willard and John W. Marr, "Effects of Human Activities on Alpine Tundra Ecosystems in Rocky Mountain National Park, Colorado," *Biological Conservation* 2,4 (1970), 257–265; and Willard and Marr, "Recovery of Alpine Tundra Under Protection After Damage by Human Activities in the Rocky Mountain National Park of Colorado," *Biological Conservation* 3,3 (1971), 181–190.

20. Description taken from Karl Hess, "Rocky Times in the Rocky Mountain National Park," *Liberty* 5,3 (January 1992), 31–32. This brief essay, published at the urging of my friend, William Bradford, was my first—albeit very rough—cut at portraying the ecological problems of Rocky Mountain.

21. David R. Stevens, "Bibliography — Technical Publications, Theses, and Scientific Papers," Rocky Mountain National Park, Estes Park (24 October 1991).

22. During the three years (1988–1991), I worked in the park preparing the vegetation inventory for the National Park Service, I became acquainted with researchers from Colorado State University and the University of Colorado. At the same time I enjoyed hours of conversation with Rocky Mountain's science staff. Time and again I heard

and recorded serious misgivings by all parties concerning the management and ecological condition of Rocky Mountain. Much of the information included in the following pages comes from those conversations.

CHAPTER 2: BEASTS OF PLUNDER

1. Neal G. Guse, Jr., "Administrative History of an Elk Herd," M.S. thesis, Colorado State University, Fort Collins (1966), 14, 20. The Forest Service organized and directed the two transplants, but much of the money to pay for the transportation of the Yellowstone elk consisted of private funds raised by the Estes Park Protective and Improvement Association.

2. Estes Park *Trail,* 30 October 1931.

3. Guse, "Administrative History," 27.

4. Ibid., 28.

5. Joseph S. Dixon, "Report on Needed Winter Range for Big Game in Rocky Mountain National Park," Rocky Mountain National Park, Estes Park (30 June 1931), 5.

6. Guse, "Administrative History," 32.

7. H.W. Steinhoff, "Certain Aspects of the Ecology of the Ponderosa Pine Community as Revealed by a Study of Twelve Small Exclosures in Rocky Mountain National Park," Report No. 427, Rocky Mountain National Park, Estes Park (May 1962), 1. Steinhoff's estimate of 1,210 may be inaccurate. David R. Stevens, formerly a research biologist at Rocky Mountain National Park, reported the 1939 estimated elk population to be 900 head. However, Stevens also reported the estimated elk population for 1938 to be 1,100. If the latter estimate is correct, Steinhoff's count may not be very far off. See David R. Stevens, "The Deer and Elk of Rocky Mountain National Park—A 10-Year Study," RMNO-N-13, Rocky Mountain National Park, Estes Park (October 1980), 35.

8. Guse, "Administrative History," 33.

9. Ibid.; and Fred Mallery Packard, "A Study of the Deer and Elk Herds of Rocky Mountain National Park, Colorado," *Journal of Mammalogy* 28,1 (February 1947), 11–12.

10. Harold Ratcliff, "Winter Range Conditions in Rocky Mountain National Park," in *Transactions of the Sixth North American Wildlife Conference* (1941), 132–139.

11. Guse, "Administrative History," 34–35. Ratcliff ("Winter Range Conditions in Rocky Mountain National Park," 138) placed the estimated winter range carrying capacity at 530 head.

12. Guse, "Administrative History," 36.

13. Steinhoff, "Certain Aspects of the Ecology of the Ponderosa Pine Community," 2.

14. Stevens, "The Deer and Elk of Rocky Mountain National Park," 35. Steinhoff's figures (Steinhoff, "Certain Aspects of the Ecology of the Ponderosa Pine Community") for the period 1944–1961 show an estimated average herd size of almost 800, considerably above the 400-head estimated carrying capacity for the park's winter range.

15. Guse, "Administrative History," 46.

16. Ibid., 45.

17. Robert F. Buttery, "Range Conditions and Trends Resulting from Winter Concentrations of Elk in Rocky Mountain National Park, Colorado," M.S. thesis, Colorado Agricultural College, Fort Collins (March 1955), 103–105.

18. Guse, "Administrative History," 38.

19. Hillory A. Tolson, memorandum to regional director, Region II, 17 January 1946, quoted in Guse, "Administrative History," 40.

20. Stevens, "The Deer and Elk of Rocky Mountain National Park," 15. Elk removal ended in 1968 with the trapping and relocation of 175 animals.

21. Neal G. Guse, Jr., et al., "Rocky Mountain Cooperative Elk Studies—Preliminary Report 1962–1963," Rocky Mountain National Park, Roosevelt National Forest, and Colorado Game, Fish, and Parks Department (1 April 1964), 40–41.

22. Stevens, "The Deer and Elk of Rocky Mountain National Park," 51. The 16, 316-acre figure used by the Park Service indicates the physical dimensions of the winter range on the east side of the park. However, not all of that acreage is usable or desired habitat for elk. The figure of 4,425 acres indicates "key" elk winter range—winter range that is most heavily used by elk. Whereas the geographical size

of winter range for elk is 16,316 acres, the ecological size—the portion used primarily for shelter and food—is one-quarter that amount.

23. R. Bruce Gill, "Management Recommendations, Rocky Mountain National Park Cooperative Elk Study," Project No. W-38-R-22, Rocky Mountain National Park, Roosevelt National Forest, and Colorado Game, Fish, and Parks Department (July 1968), 359–360.

24. Ibid., 360–361.

25. Ibid., 363.

26. Stevens, "The Deer and Elk of Rocky Mountain National Park," 17.

27. David R. Stevens, "Effect of Elk on Vegetation in Rocky Mountain National Park," Rocky Mountain National Park, Estes Park (November 1979), 1; and Glen F. Cole, "An Ecological Rationale for the Natural or Artificial Regulation of Native Ungulates in Parks," in *Transactions of the Thirty-Sixth North American Wildlife and Natural Resources Conference* (Washington, D.C.: Wildlife Management Institute, 1971), 417–425.

28. The natural regulation hypothesis put forward by Cole stems from research by Graeme Caughley in New Zealand and A.R.E. Sinclair in Tanzania. Critics have challenged the applicability of that research to the regulation of herbivore populations in North America. See Graeme Caughley, "Eruption of Ungulate Populations with Emphasis on Himalayan Thar in New Zealand," *Ecology* 53,1 (1970), 53–72; and A.R.E. Sinclair, *The African Buffalo: A Study of Resource Limitation of Populations* (Chicago: University of Chicago Press, 1977).

29. National Park Service, "Policy Statement—Elk Management in Rocky Mountain National Park," Rocky Mountain National Park, Estes Park (1968).

30. Cole, "An Ecological Rationale for the Natural or Artificial Regulation of Native Ungulates in Parks." The application of natural regulation to Yellowstone National Park is described in Alston Chase, *Playing God in Yellowstone: The Destruction of America's First National Park* (Boston: The Atlantic Monthly Press, 1986); and Charles E. Kay, "Yellowstone's Northern Elk Herd: A Critical Evaluation of the 'Natural Regulation' Paradigm," Ph.D. diss., Utah State University, Logan (1990).

31. Rocky Mountain's experiment in natural regulation can be thought of as a compromised hybrid of Yellowstone's earlier program of natural control and its present policy of natural regulation (see Kay, "Yellowstone's Northern Elk Herd"). Under natural control, elk numbers were expected to be balanced with the food supply through predation by wolves and other natural carnivores. Because of Rocky Mountain's small size and the urban development surrounding it, hunters are the necessary substitute for natural predators. Hunting of elk along the park's boundaries in turn supplements the natural regulating effects of severe weather and limited food supplies—environmental variables that in larger ecosystems, such as Yellowstone, should in theory be sufficient in themselves to bring the elk population into ecological balance with the land.

32. Interviews with David R. Stevens, research biologist, Rocky Mountain National Park, Estes Park (21 November 1991 and 13 January 1992). In addition to these interviews, I spent hours in conversation with Stevens while I was engaged in my vegetation study of Rocky Mountain (1988–1991). It should be noted that Stevens does not consider the park's elk policy to be natural regulation. Technically he is correct, since Rocky Mountain's policy is a hybrid of natural control and natural regulation—at least as they are defined and practiced in Yellowstone National Park. Nonetheless, I believe that "natural regulation" is an appropriate and useful term to describe what is currently happening in the park. The term is also used in the park's 1968 policy statement on elk.

33. Stevens, "The Deer and Elk of Rocky Mountain National Park," 35.

34. Interviews with Stevens; David R. Stevens, "Ungulate Winter Habitat Conditions and Management," Rocky Mountain National Park, Estes Park (reports for 1980 through 1990); and Stevens, "Ungulate Winter Habitat Conditions and Management" (1990), 5.

35. N.T. Hobbs, D.L. Baker, J.E. Ellis, D.M. Swift, and R.A. Green, "Energy- and Nitrogen-Based Estimates of Elk Winter-Range Carrying Capacity," *Journal of Wildlife Management* 46,1 (1982), 12. See also Hobbs, "Winter Diet Quality and Nutritional Status of Elk in the Upper Montane Zone, Colorado," Ph.D. diss., Colorado State University, Fort Collins (1979).

36. Interview with Gene Schoonveldt, senior big game biologist, Colorado Division of Wildlife, Fort Collins (21 April 1992).

37. Interview with Schoonveldt.

38. Stevens, "The Deer and Elk of Rocky Mountain National Park," 44, 151. Harvest figures for 1980 through 1990 had not yet been published when this was written.

39. Gill, "Management Recommendations," 360–361.

40. George D. Bear, "Seasonal Distribution and Population Characteristics of Elk in Estes Valley, Colorado," Special Report No. 65, Colorado Division of Wildlife (April 1989), 11. Emphasis added.

41. George D. Bear and R.A. Green, "Colorado Division of Wildlife Research Report," W-126-R-3, Big Game Investigations, Elk Population and Ecology Studies, Colorado Division of Wildlife (July 1980), 221.

42. Ibid., 11–12.

43. Stevens, "Ungulate Winter Habitat Conditions and Management," 1990.

44. David R. Stevens, "Ungulate Habitat Condition and Trend," ROMO-N-08a, Rocky Mountain National Park, Estes Park (1982), 3.

45. Stevens, "The Deer and Elk of Rocky Mountain National Park," 145.

46. Interview with Henry E. McCutchen, wildlife biologist, Rocky Mountain National Park, Estes Park (28 June 1990); and interview with Schoonveldt.

47. Empirical evidence of vegetation condition and trend in Rocky Mountain National Park is essential, given the uncertainty about elk numbers on the winter range. This uncertainty is highlighted by a 1989 report in the *Journal of Wildlife Management* that downwardly revised elk population estimates made in the early 1980s. See G.D. Bear, G.C. White, and L.H. Carpenter, "Evaluation of Aerial Mark-Resighting Estimates of Elk Population," *Journal of Wildlife Management* 53,4 (1989), 908–915.

48. Stevens, "The Deer and Elk of Rocky Mountain National Park," 140.

49. U.S. Department of the Interior, *An Ecological Characterization of Rocky Mountain and Subalpine Wetlands,* U.S. Fish and Wildlife Service, Biological Report (Washington, D.C.: Government Printing Office, September 1986), 231.

50. National Park Service, "Policy Statement," 1968.

51. Ronald A. Green, "Elk Habitat Selection and Activity Patterns in Rocky Mountain National Park, Colorado," M.S. thesis, Colorado State University, Fort Collins (fall 1982), 129–131.

52. E. Mills, *The Rocky Mountain National Park*; and Buchholtz, *Rocky Mountain National Park*.

53. Fred Mallery Packard, "Wildlife and Aspen in Rocky Mountain National Park, Colorado," *Ecology* 23,4 (October 1942), 481.

54. Packard, "Wildlife and Aspen," 480.

55. Frederic E. Nichols, "Aspen Ecology in Eastern Northcentral Colorado," M.S. thesis, Colorado State University, Fort Collins (spring 1986), 58–59. Nichols revisited several of Packard's study sites and found "very few living aspen stems . . . [and] in the vicinity of these sites, all exhibit elk incisor scars."

56. Leslie W. Gysel, "An Ecological Study of the Winter Range of Elk and Mule Deer in the Rocky Mountain National Park," *Journal of Forestry* 58,9 (September 1959), 699–700.

57. Ibid., 699.

58. Green, "Elk Habitat Selection," 131.

59. Buttery, "Range Conditions and Trends," 90, 93, 99.

60. Evaluating the success or failure of natural regulation requires credible scientific data. Published data are not abundant. Only eight dissertations and two dozen journal articles touch on the subject. For that reason, the bulk of data cited in this chapter is unpublished, drawn mostly from the archives of the National Park Service at Rocky Mountain. Over forty reports, most based on original data collected between 1968 and 1990, stand behind the conclusions reached in this chapter. They are cited repeatedly.

Admittedly, these forty-plus reports have not been refereed, but their data are extensive, compelling, and not contradicted by any countervailing scientific source. Indeed, the information on which management of public lands in general is based is drawn mostly from collections of unpublished data and agency reports. There is virtually no other source of information. We rely on federal agencies to study and monitor public lands, be they parks, forests, or grazing lands. Courts rely on agency data to make decisions; policy makers to draft policy; resource managers to make management decisions. And environmental groups look to agency data to determine how well those agencies have done their job. When Forest Service data show 80 or 90 percent utilization of willows or grass by cattle, reasonable people do not contest the data or request peer-reviewed papers to determine whether overgrazing is in fact occurring.

The same principle holds for Rocky Mountain National Park. More than two decades of systematic and intensive data collection, bolstered by even more years of spot data collection, provide an impressive body of evidence. Moreover, the soundness of that data is corroborated by the scientists most familiar with Rocky Mountain and by nearly three-quarters of a century of scientific reports and publications. Together, over seventy sources of documentation were consulted for this chapter alone, none of which has been refuted. Finally, I bring my own expertise to the interpretation of these data, expertise based on seven years of studying and writing about the vegetation of Rocky Mountain National Park and the forest lands lying adjacent to its borders.

61. Vegetation data collected by Stevens indicate ecological deterioration in terms of declining diversity of plant communities. Under natural conditions, nothing close to the ongoing widespread eradication of major Rocky Mountain plant communities would be expected.

62. Nichols, "Aspen Ecology," 59.

63. Charles E. Olmsted, "Aspen Utilization by Large Herbivores in Rocky Mountain National Park and its Implications for Management," Rocky Mountain Park, Estes Park (1977), 2, 11, 12.

64. Stevens, "The Deer and Elk of Rocky Mountain National Park," 125.

65. Cole, "An Ecological Rationale for the Natural or Artificial Regulation of Native Ungulates in Parks": and D.B. Houston, "Ecosystems of National Parks," *Science* 172 (1971), 648–651.

66. A.A. Beetle, "Range Survey in Teton County, Wyoming. Part IV—Quaking Aspen," University of Wyoming Agricultural Experiment Station, Laramie (1974), 28.

67. Charles E. Olmsted, "The Effect of Large Herbivores on Aspen in Rocky Mountain National Park," Ph.D. diss., University of Colorado, Boulder (1977), 136.

68. Stevens, "The Deer and Elk of Rocky Mountain National Park," 120.

69. Excerpts taken from David R. Stevens, "Ungulate Winter Habitat Study," Rocky Mountain National Park, Estes Park (reports for

1968–1990).

70. Because aspen is a successional species, many of the aspen stands in Rocky Mountain that are decadent today would have disappeared even without the influence of elk. However, in the absence of excessive elk numbers, aspen stands would likely have renewed themselves in some areas and in others would have become established for the first time. A dynamic and shifting landscape pattern of juvenile and mature aspen stands would have prevailed where today mostly mature and dying aspen dominate.

71. Interview with park naturalist (unnamed by request), Green Mountain residence area, Rocky Mountain National Park, Grand Lake (12 August 1990); and interviews with Stevens.

72. David R. Stevens, "Ungulate Winter Habitat Study," Rocky Mountain National Park, Estes Park (1969). "Dis-climax successional stage" refers to an arrested stage of vegetation development, a peculiar and persisting form of plant community where species composition and total productivity are maintained at a level other than climax by the influence of an external factor, in this case elk.

73. Excerpts taken from Stevens, "Ungulate Winter Habitat Study" (reports for 1968 through 1990). The term "zootic climax" refers to the species makeup of a plant community that is persistently maintained by animal grazing or some other animal influence.

74. Interview with Clinton Wasser, professor emeritus, Colorado State University, Fort Collins (23 April 1992).

75. Stevens, "Ungulate Winter Habitat Conditions and Management," Rocky Mountain National Park, Estes Park (1989).

76. Interviews with Stevens and McCutchen.

77. Rocky Mountain National Park, "Policy Statement," 1968.

78. Ibid.

79. Harold M. Ratcliff and Lowell Sumner, "National Park Wildlife Ranges," in *Transactions of the Tenth North American Wildlife Conference* (1945), 246–250.

80. David R. Stevens, "Impact of Elk on Alpine Tundra in Rocky Mountain National Park," in C.L. Jackson and M.A. Schuster, eds., *Proceedings: High Altitude Revegetation Workshop No. 4,* Colorado State University Information Series No. 42 (Fort Collins: Colorado State University, 1980), 228–241.

81. Clait E. Braun, David R. Stevens, Kenneth M. Giesen, and Cynthia P. Melcher, "Elk, White-tailed Ptarmigan and Willow Relationships: A Management Dilemma in Rocky Mountain National Park," in *Transactions of the Fifty-sixth North American Wildlife and Natural Resources Conference* (1991), 82–83.

82. E. Mills, *The Rocky Mountain National Park*, 67.

83. E.A. Warren, "Notes on the Beaver Colonies in the Longs Peak Region of Estes Park, Colorado," *Roosevelt Wildlife Annuals* 1,2 (1926), 193–234.

84. Fred M. Packard, "A Survey of the Beaver Population of Rocky Mountain National Park, Colorado," *Journal of Mammalogy* 28,3 (August 1947), 221.

85. Comparison between 1926 and 1940 beaver census data points to this conclusion.

86. David R. Stevens and Stanley Christianson, "Beaver Populations on East Slope of Rocky Mountain National Park," special report, Rocky Mountain National Park, Estes Park (1980), 5.

87. Ibid., 6.

88. Nancy Jacobson, David R. Stevens, and Mike Arlanskas, "Beaver Population Survey 1981," special report, Rocky Mountain National Park, Estes Park (1981).

89. January 1992 interview with Stevens.

90. Interviews with Cathy Green, wildlife biologist, Colorado Division of Wildlife, Denver (10 April 1992), and Gene Schoonveldt, senior big game biologist, Colorado Division of Wildlife, Fort Collins (21 April 1992).

91. U.S. Department of the Interior, U.S. Fish and Wildlife Service, *Restoring America's Wildlife* (Washington, D.C.: U.S. Government Printing Office, 1987).

92. Packard, "A Survey of the Beaver Population," 227.

93. Robert L. Hoover, "Beaver Ecology in the Longs Peak Area of Colorado," M.S. thesis, Colorado A & M College, Fort Collins (March 1955), 236; and Don J. Neff, "Relationships of Fire and Forest Succession to Beaver Environment on Roaring Fork, Estes Park, Colorado, "M.S. thesis, Colorado A and M College, Fort Collins (1955).

94. Packer, "A Survey of the Beaver Population," 227.

95. Gysel, "An Ecological Study of the Winter Range," 699.

96. Packard, "A Survey of the Beaver Population," 221.

97. Stevens and Christiansen, "Beaver Populations on East Slope of Rocky Mountain National Park," 5.

98. James Gleick, "Species Vanishing from Many Parks," *The New York Times* (3 February 1987).

99. Robert B. Allen, Robert K. Peet, and William L. Baker, "Gradient Analysis of Latitudinal Variation in Southern Rocky Mountain Forests," *Journal of Biogeography* 18 (1991), 123–139; Robert B. Allen and Robert K. Peet, "Gradient Analysis of Forests of the Sangre de Cristo Range, Colorado," *Canadian Journal of Botany* 68 (1990), 193–201; Robert K. Peet, "Latitudinal Variation in Southern Rocky Mountain Forests," *Journal of Biogeography* 5 (1978), 275–289; and Robert K. Peet, "Forest Vegetation of the Colorado Front Range: Patterns of Species Diversity," *Vegetatio* 37 (1978), 65–78.

CHAPTER 3: LANDSCAPES OF FIRE

1. Robert K. Peet, "Forests of the Rocky Mountains," in Michael G. Barbour and William Dwight Billings, eds., *North American Terrestrial Vegetation* (Cambridge: Cambridge University Press, 1986), 69, 95.

2. Thomas T. Veblen and Diane C. Lorenz, *The Colorado Front Range: A Century of Ecological Change* (Salt Lake City: University of Utah Press, 1991), 24.

3. Frederic E. Clements, "The Life History of Lodgepole Burn Forests," U.S. Department of Agriculture, Forest Service Bulletin 79, Washington, D.C. (1910), 8.

4. National Park Service, "Fire Management Plan for Rocky Mountain National Park, Colorado," Rocky Mountain National Park, Estes Park (January 1992), 8.

5. Ibid.

6. Ibid.

7. David B. Butts, "Fire Management in Rocky Mountain National Park," in *Proceedings of the Tall Timbers Fire Ecology Conference No. 14 and*

Intermountain Fire Research Council Fire and Land Management Symposium (Tallahassee, Fla: Tall Timbers Research Station, 1976), 62. As will become evident, these estimates of natural fire occurrence may be too conservative—a reflection of the pervasive effect of modern fire suppression after an era when fire frequency and intensity were abnormally high.

8. Harry B. Clagg, "Fire Ecology in High-Elevation Forests in Colorado," M.S. thesis, Colorado State University, Fort Collins (May 1975), 84.

9. Kirk M. Rowdabaugh, "The Role of Fire in the Ponderosa Pine–Mixed Conifer Ecosystems," M.S. thesis, Colorado State University, Fort Collins (Summer 1978), 96.

10. R.D. Laven, P.N. Omi, J.G. Wyant, and A.S. Pinkerton, "Interpretation of Fire Scar Data from a Ponderosa Pine Ecosystem in the Central Rocky Mountains, Colorado," in *Proceedings of the Fire History Workshop,* General Technical Report RM-81 (Fort Collins, Colo: Rocky Mountain Forest and Range Experiment Station, 1980), 47.

11. Thomas V. Skinner, "Background Data for Natural Fire Management in Rocky Mountain National Park," professional paper, Colorado State University, Fort Collins (November 1987), v; Veblen and Lorenz, *The Colorado Front Range,* 25; Peet, "Forests of the Rocky Mountains," 70; Thomas V. Skinner and Richard D. Laven, "Final Report: Background Data for Natural Fire Management in Rocky Mountain National Park," Department of Forest and Wood Sciences, Colorado State University, Fort Collins (15 November 1984); and interview with Richard D. Laven, professor of fire ecology, Department of Forest and Wood Sciences, Colorado State University, Fort Collins (1 April 1992). Although Peet indicates that crown fire frequency in lower-elevation lodgepole pine can be as low as 50 years, Laven's data suggest that a minimum fire frequency of 150 years is more common for the majority of Rocky Mountain's lodgepole pine communities.

12. Veblen and Lorenz, *The Colorado Front Range,* 25; and M.F. Crane, "Fire Ecology of Rocky Mountain Region Forest Habitat Types," final report, U.S. Department of Agriculture, Forest Service Region Two, Missoula, Mont. (15 May 1982).

13. Veblen and Lorenz, *The Colorado Front Range,* 25; and Crane, "Fire Ecology of Rocky Mountain Region," 136. For readers unfamiliar with the technical terms "stand" and "seral," brief definitions are in order. A forest stand or a stand of trees is simply a homogeneous grouping of trees—a "slice" of a much larger forest that is identifiable because of biological, ecological, physical, or management traits. "Seral" refers to a successional stage of vegetation. A seral stand is a grouping of trees that will eventually be replaced by a climax stand—a stand of trees that will persist in the absence of disturbance and that are the optimal plant community for the immediate environment.

14. Butts, "Fire Management in Rocky Mountain National Park," 62.

15. Crane, "Fire Ecology of Rocky Mountain Forest Habitat Types."

16. Veblen and Lorenz, *The Colorado Front Range,* 25.

17. Thomas V. Skinner and Richard D. Laven, "A Fire History of the Longs Peak Region of Rocky Mountain National Park," Department of Forest and Wood Sciences, Colorado State University, Fort Collins (January 1983); and Rowdabaugh, "The Role of Fire in the Ponderosa Pine-Mixed Conifer Ecosystems."

18. National Park Service, "Fire Management Plan for Rocky Mountain National Park, Colorado," 8.

19. Veblen and Lorenz, *The Colorado Front Range,* 25.

20. Clements, "The Life History of Lodgepole Burn Forests," 8.

21. Buchholtz, *Rocky Mountain National Park,* 171.

22. Veblen and Lorenz, *The Colorado Front Range,* 25.

23. Skinner and Laven, "A Fire History of the Longs Peak Region of Rocky Mountain National Park," 72.

24. Butts, "Fire Management in Rocky Mountain National Park," 62.

25. Clagg, "Fire Ecology in High-Elevation Forests in Colorado," 84.

26. Rowdabaugh, "The Role of Fire in the Ponderosa Pine-Mixed Conifer Ecosystems," 96.

27. National Park Service, "Fire Management Plan for Rocky Mountain National Park Colorado," 8.

28. Butts, "Fire Management in Rocky Mountain National Park," 62; Buchholtz, *Rocky Mountain National Park,* 199; and Skinner, "Back-

ground Data for Natural Fire Management in Rocky Mountain National Park," 7–8.

29. National Park Service, "Fire Management Plan for Rocky Mountain National Park," 8.

30. Peet, "Forests of the Rocky Mountains," 95.

31. Butts, "Fire Management in Rocky Mountain National Park," 62.

32. National Park Service, "Fire Management Plan for Rocky Mountain National Park, Colorado," 9.

33. Interview with Laven.

34. Veblen and Lorenz, *The Colorado Front Range,* 175.

35. Clements, "The Life History of Lodgepole Burn Forests," 9.

36. National Park Service, "Fire Management Plan for Rocky Mountain National Park, Colorado," 9.

37. Ibid.

38. Interview with Edward W. Mogren, professor emeritus, Department of Forest and Wood Sciences, Colorado State University, Fort Collins (20 January 1992); interview with Laven; and National Park Service, "Fire Management Plan for Rocky Mountain National Park, Colorado."

39. Interview with Craig Axtell, chief of resources management, Rocky Mountain National Park, Estes Park (25 March 1992). In Axtell's judgment, low-elevation fires originating outside the park's boundaries were historically crucial to the fire ecology of Rocky Mountain's high-elevation forests.

40. Jack S. Barrows, E.W. Mogren, Kirk Rowdabaugh, and Richard Yancik, "The Role of Fire in Ponderosa Pine and Mixed Conifer Ecosystems," final report, Rocky Mountain National Park, Estes Park (December 1977), 15.

41. Barrows, "The Role of Fire in Ponderosa Pine and Mixed Conifer Ecosystems," 16.

42. Ibid.

43. National Park Service, "Fire Management Plan for Rocky Mountain National Park, Colorado," 10.

44. Veblen and Lorenz, *The Colorado Front Range,* 140.

45. Karl Hess, "Final Report: Description and Evaluation of Cover Types

in the Rocky Mountain National Park," Rocky Mountain National Park, Estes Park (January 1991), 64–67, 71–73.

46. Aspen on Colorado's Western Slope, including the west side of Rocky Mountain, are considered by some ecologists to be persistent rather than successional, given appropriate soil, moisture, and temperature conditions. See Karl Hess, "Phyto-Edaphic Study of Habitat Types of the Arapaho-Roosevelt National Forest," Ph.D. diss., Colorado State University, Fort Collins (1981); Karl Hess and Robert R. Alexander, "Forest Vegetation of the Arapaho and Roosevelt National Forests in Central Colorado: A Habitat Type Classification," U.S. Forest Service, Rocky Mountain Forest and Range Experiment Station Paper RM-266, Fort Collins (1986); and Karl Hess and Clinton H. Wasser, "The Grassland, Shrubland, and Forestland Habitat Types of the White River–Arapaho National Forest," U.S. Forest Service, Rocky Mountain Forest and Range Experiment Station, Fort Collins (1982).

47. Interview with Laven. My research indicates that aspen is most endangered east of the Continental Divide, where fire dependency is a near-universal condition for aspen forests. West of the Divide, aspen is not nearly as abundant. Among the stands that do exist on the western side of the park, some may have the ability to maintain themselves in the absence of fire. See Hess and Alexander, "Forest Vegetation of the Arapaho and Roosevelt National Forests in Central Colorado: A Habitat Type Classification": Hess and Wasser, "The Grassland, Shrubland, and Forestland Habitat Types of the White River–Arapaho National Forests": and George R. Hoffman and Robert R. Alexander, "Forest Vegetation of the Routt National Forest in Northwestern Colorado: A Habitat Type Classification," Research Paper RM-221, U.S. Forest Service, Rocky Mountain Forest and Range Experiment Station, Fort Collins (1980).

48. Don J. Neff, "Relationships of Fire and Forest Succession to Beaver Environment on Roaring Fork, Estes Park, Colorado," M.S. thesis, Colorado A & M College, Fort Collins (1955).

49. Albert J. Parker and Kathleen C. Parker, "Comparative Successional Roles of Trembling Aspen and Lodgepole Pine in the Southern Rocky Mountains," *Great Basin Naturalist* 43,3 (July 1983), 453.

50. Frederic E. Nichols, "Aspen Ecology in Eastern Northcentral Colorado," M.S. thesis, Colorado State University, Fort Collins (Spring 1986), 47.

51. Ibid., 64–67.

52. Interview with Joyce Gellhorn, ecologist, Boulder, Colo. (2 April 1992). Gellhorn is working with Rocky Mountain staff in a cooperative study on plant recovery and succession at the 1,050-acre Ouzel fire site.

53. Many lodgepole pine forests in Rocky Mountain can be considered persistent climax vegetation—particularly on drier and warmer mid- and high-elevation sites. See William H. Moir, "The Lodgepole Pine Zone in Colorado," *American Midland Naturalist* 81 (1969), 331–340.

54. Clements, "The Life History of Lodgepole Burn Forests," 53.

55. Ibid.

56. Thomas Franklin and Richard D. Laven, "Fire Influences on Central Rocky Mountain Lodgepole Pine Stand Structure and Composition," in *Proceedings of the Seventeenth Tall Timbers Fire Ecology Conference* (Tallahassee, Fla.: Tall Timbers Research Station, 1989), 190–191.

57. The importance of disturbance and disturbance processes (like fire) to ecosystem health is basic to *patch ecology*. Now at the forefront of ecological thinking, patch ecology is described in S.A. Picket and P.S. White, *The Ecology of Natural Disturbance and Patch Dynamics* (New York: Academic Press, 1985).

58. Veblen and Lorenz, *The Colorado Front Range,* 138–143.

59. Ibid., 175; Peet, "Forests of the Rocky Mountains," 70; and Hess, "Description and Evaluation of Cover Types in the Rocky Mountain National Park," 57–60. Dramatic visual evidence of the destruction of Douglas-fir is in Veblen and Lorenz, *The Colorado Front Range.*

60. Plant succession in budworm-infested stands will occur without fire, but it will take a somewhat different course.

61. The ecology and management of western spruce budworm is comprehensively treated in Martha A. Brookes, Robert W. Campbell, J.J. Colbert, Russel G. Mitchell, and R.W. Stark, eds., *Western Spruce Budworm,* Forest Service Technical Bulletin No. 1694 (Washington, D.C.: U.S. Department of Agriculture, 1987); and Thomas W. Swetnam and Ann M. Lynch, "A Tree-Ring Reconstruction of Western Spruce Budworm History in the Southern Rocky Mountains," *Forest Science* 35,4 (1989), 962–986. Also it should be noted that

periodic local disturbances and the resulting patchwork of vegetation are deemed essential by modern ecologists for the maintenance of dynamic ecological systems. Details on patch dynamics and disturbance ecology can be found in Picket and White, *The Ecology of Natural Disturbance and Patch Dynamics.*

62. Brookes et al., *Western Spruce Budworm,* 16.

63. Veblen and Lorenz, *The Colorado Front Range,* 128–137.

64. November 1991 interview with Stevens; and Stevens, "Ungulate Winter Habitat Conditions and Management" (1968 through 1990). In addition, heavy grazing by elk that reduces herb competition with seedling trees may also be a contributing factor to tree invasion of meadows at higher elevations (interview with W.H. Moir, research ecologist, U.S Forest Service, Rocky Mountain Forest and Range Experiment Station, Fort Collins).

65. Interview with Laven.

66. Interviews with Laven, Stevens (November 1991), and McCutchen (June 1990). Conflagration in Rocky Mountain would entail ecological and sociological consequences far greater than those associated with the Yellowstone fires of 1988. Not only is Rocky Mountain a crucial plant and wildlife sanctuary in the midst of residential and commercial development, but the entire east side of the park is bordered by an expanding urban environment. A major fire could generate disproportionate disturbances to, and losses of, plant, animal, and human life.

67. National Park Service, "Fire Management Plan for Rocky Mountain National Park," 10.

68. Veblen and Lorenz, *The Colorado Front Range,* 175.

69. These observations were made while the author was collecting data for the Park Service–commissioned study of Rocky Mountain National Park cover types (Hess, "Description and Evaluation of Cover Types in the Rocky Mountain National Park").

70. Veblen and Lorenz, *The Colorado Front Range,* 175.

71. Laven describes the future fire danger in Rocky Mountain National Park in similar terms: "Vast acreages of relatively even-aged lodgepole pine forests will be susceptible to high intensity, difficult to control, crown fire" (letter from Richard D. Laven, professor of forest sciences, Colorado State University, to Karl Hess, 20 January 1993).

72. See 16 United States Code, Section 1, 1982, commonly referred to as the "Organic Act" of the National Park Service. It mandates the Park Service "to conserve the scenery and the natural and historic objects and the wild life therein and to provide for the enjoyment of the same in such manner and by such means as will leave them unimpaired for the enjoyment of future generations." Federal courts have interpreted the "Organic Act" to be a mandate for preserving national parks in a natural state. See also United States District Court for the District of Columbia, "National Rifle Association of America, *et al.,* Plaintiffs, v. J. Craig Potter, Acting Assistant Secretary for Fish and Wildlife and Parks, *et al.,* Defendants," Memorandum and Order, Civil Action No. 84-1348, 24 February 1986.

73. Interviews with Stevens (January 1992) and McCutchen. Stevens cited twenty-two years of data collection to back up his pessimistic conclusion regarding the apparent decline of plant community and landscape diversity in Rocky Mountain National Park (Stevens, "Ungulate Winter Habitat Study" [1968 through 1990]). His specific concerns focused on biological diversity within elk winter range. McCutchen was also concerned with species diversity and ecosystem health on the park's winter range. He attributed Rocky Mountain's loss of plant community diversity on winter range to the park's commitment to natural regulation, a theory of management that, he believed, had wrongly reduced the role of park managers to that of passive custodians. McCutchen also stressed the adverse effects of Rocky Mountain's fire suppression policy on landscape diversity at higher elevations.

74. Hess, "Phyto-Edaphic Study of Habitat Types of the Arapaho-Roosevelt National Forest"; and Hess and Alexander, "Forest Vegetation of the Arapaho and Roosevelt National Forests in Central Colorado: A Habitat Type Classification."

75. Hess, "Description and Evaluation of Cover Types in the Rocky Mountain National Park," 35.

76. Colorado blue spruce communities in the central and southern Rocky Mountains are discussed in Hess and Alexander, "Forest Vegetation of the Arapaho and Roosevelt National Forests in Central Colorado: A Habitat Type Classification"; George R. Hoffman and Robert R. Alexander, "Forest Vegetation of the White River National Forest in Western Colorado: A Habitat Type Classification," U.S. Forest Service, Rocky Mountain Forest and Range Experiment Sta-

tion Research Paper RM-249, Fort Collins (August 1983); and William H. Moir and John A. Ludwig, "A Classification of Spruce-Fir and Mixed Conifer Habitat Types of Arizona and New Mexico," U.S. Forest Service, Rocky Mountain Forest and Range Experiment Station Research Paper RM-207, Fort Collins (July 1979). Reference to Colorado blue spruce in Rocky Mountain National Park appears in Robert K. Peet, "Forest Vegetation of the East Slope of the Northern Colorado Front Range," Ph.D. diss., Cornell University (1975). These studies indicate that the elevation range of Colorado blue spruce communities varies from between 7,800 and 9,800 feet in northern Arizona and New Mexico to between 7,500 and 8,800 feet in northern Colorado.

77. My knowledge of the environmental problems facing Colorado blue spruce in Rocky Mountain National Park comes from two sources. First, when I inquired where I might find samples of blue spruce communities to examine for my Park Service–commissioned study of cover types in Rocky Mountain, park staff informed me that few existed and that even fewer existed in anything approaching pristine condition. Second, my three years of inventorying and mapping the vegetation of Rocky Mountain exposed me to the few stands that still existed and the types of disturbances affecting them. See Hess, "Description and Evaluation of Cover Types in the Rocky Mountain National Park."

78. George Hoffman and Robert Alexander ("Forest Vegetation of the White River National Forest in Western Colorado: A Habitat Type Classification") found most stands of Colorado blue spruce in the White River National Forest to "have been disturbed; and in many places only a few scattered *Picea pungens* are left, surrounded by a rank growth of heliophytic shrubs and herbaceous vegetation" (p. 21). I found similar signs of disturbance in blue spruce stands in the area of the Roosevelt National Forest that lies adjacent to Rocky Mountain National Park (Hess, "Phyto-Edaphic Study of Habitat Types of the Arapaho-Roosevelt National Forest, Colorado," p. 261). Given the similarities in the early histories of the two forests and the park, it is reasonable to assume that Colorado blue spruce met a similar fate in all three; that in all three blue spruce communities that had once thrived were later disturbed and frequently eliminated by human presence.

79. Blue spruce communities are highly resilient and very responsive to

restoration measures. In particular, understory vegetation can recover to its natural potential in just a few years with proper protection. A prime example of blue spruce restoration occurred in the Blue Lakes area of northern New Mexico, in Carson National Forest. While under the control and management of the U.S. Forest Service, the area's blue spruce stands were heavily impacted by concentrated human use in and around developed picnic facilities. In the 1970s the entire area was transferred to the Rio Pueblo de Taos. Because the area had religious significance to the people of the Pueblo, the picnic facilities in the blue spruce stands were dismantled and removed and concentrated human use was eliminated. Within a few years, the site returned to near-climax conditions (interview with Moir).

80. January 1992 interview with Stevens. Man-made drainage ditches are being removed from Big Meadows to restore natural water conditions.

81. The Range Science Department of Colorado State University is currently receiving National Park Service funding for reclamation and restoration of alpine areas disturbed by human activity.

82. I learned of the importation of Colorado blue spruce to Russia during my graduate residence at Colorado State University. Faculty in the Botany Department regularly shared this anecdote with students to stir loyalty to and pride in Colorado's native vegetation.

83. Interview with Henry E. McCutchen, research biologist, Rocky Mountain National Park, Estes Park (13 January 1992); and Henry E. McCutchen, "Cryptic Behavior of Black Bears (*Ursus Americanus*) in Rocky Mountain National Park, Colorado," *International Conference on Bear Research and Management* 8 (1987), 65–72.

84. Henry E. McCutchen, "Black Bear Species/Area Relationships Studied at Rocky Mountain National Park," *Park Science* 7,3 (Spring 1987), 19.

85. McCutchen, "Cryptic Behavior of Black Bears," 71.

86. McCutchen, "Black Bear Species/Area Relationships," 18–19; and McCutchen, "Cryptic Behavior of Black Bears," 71.

87. June 1990 interview with McCutchen.

88. McCutchen, "Black Bear Species/Area Relationships," 18.

CHAPTER 4: PARK IN PERIL

1. Until February 1991, three research ecologists were assigned to Rocky Mountain National Park: David R. Stevens, wildlife ecologist; Henry E. McCutchen, wildlife ecologist; and Richard Keigley, plant ecologist.

2. This is the project I carried out, which is discussed at some length in the Introduction. Also see Hess, "Description and Evaluation of Cover Types in the Rocky Mountain National Park," 1.

3. Interview with Richard Keigley, Yellowstone National Park, Gardiner, Mont. (14 October 1992).

4. Interview with Henry E. McCutchen, Northern Arizona University, Flagstaff (18 December 1992). According to McCutchen, the origins of that souring relationship reach back to earlier years when McCutchen and Keigley worked with James Thompson, then deputy director of the Rocky Mountain region under Lorraine Mintzmyer. All three men transferred to Rocky Mountain National Park at approximately the same time, with Thompson becoming superintendent. In contrast to the experiences of McCutchen and Keigley, Stevens's relationship with the park's administration began on a high note and deteriorated only in recent years (January 1992 interview with Stevens).

5. Based on interviews with Stevens (January 1992) and McCutchen (January and December 1992). By the time I had completed my research at Rocky Mountain, McCutchen was wrapping up his bear studies and Stevens was engaged almost exclusively in administrative work, specifically the oversight of research contracted to outside biologists and ecologists.

6. January 1992 interview with Stevens. When Stevens first arrived at Rocky Mountain, his working relationship with the superintendent was excellent. In recent years, that working relationship has soured. His research and reports are largely ignored by the park's administration. The recent transfer of McCutchen and Keigley confirmed what Stevens had suspected all along: an ever-widening gulf between park research and park administration. Today Stevens believes that science and scientists dedicated to monitoring vegetation and wildlife conditions are unwelcome at Rocky Mountain.

7. Interview with Laven. Laven criticized the park's administration for mishandling the 1978 Ouzel fire and failing to develop a sound fire management policy for Rocky Mountain. His criticism apparently earned him the status of persona non grata. For the past decade his ties to Rocky Mountain have been minimal to nonexistent despite his proximity to the park, his national reputation in the field of fire ecology, and his numerous writings on fire in the park.

8. Alston Chase, *Playing God in Yellowstone* (Boston: The Atlantic Monthly Press, 1986), 250–251.

9. Ibid., 252.

10. Ibid., 253–254.

11. June 1990 interview with McCutchen. McCutchen expressed general agreement with Chase's argument.

12. Henry E. McCutchen, "A History of Science in the National Park Service," draft manuscript, Rocky Mountain National Park, Estes Park (August 1990), 51, 53; and June 1990 interview with McCutchen.

13. McCutchen, "A History of Science in the National Park Service," 51.

14. June 1990 interview with McCutchen.

15. Holmes Rolston III, "Yellowstone: We Must Allow It to Change," *High Country News* 23,10 (3 June 1991), 13.

16. Ibid.

17. Harold M. Ratcliff, "Winter Range Conditions in Rocky Mountain National Park," in *Transactions of the Sixth North American Wildlife Conference* (1941), 132.

18. Stevens, "The Deer and Elk of Rocky Mountain National Park," 149.

19. Interviews with Stevens.

20. Guse, "Administrative History," 38.

21. David R. Stevens, "Ungulate Habitat Conditions and Trends," Rocky Mountain National Park, Estes Park (1975), 6.

22. Ibid., 7. Emphasis added. Wolves had been eliminated from Rocky Mountain by 1900, victims of state predator bounties and the expanding Colorado livestock industry (Stevens, "The Deer and Elk of Rocky Mountain National Park," 5).

23. David R. Stevens, "Ungulate Habitat Condition and Trend,"

ROMO-N-08a, Rocky Mountain National Park, Estes Park (1982), 3–4. Emphasis added.

24. National Park Service, "Policy Statement," 1968.

25. David R. Stevens, "Ungulate Winter Habitat Conditions and Management," ROMO-N-08a, Rocky Mountain National Park, Estes Park (1988), 6.

26. Interviews with Stevens and McCutchen (June 1990 and January 1992). Also see Edmund J. Bucknall, "Elk Population Control," *Trail and Timberline,* Colorado Mountain Club Publicaton 585 (September 1967), 172. In regard to the power of politics over the issue of elk control, Bucknall was specific; lobbying by special interest groups had precluded protection of the park: "The shooting was stopped, trapping was impossible and the range was left with nearly 500 more elk than it could adequately support. Nothing was solved, and this winter there will again be a surplus of elk on winter range."

27. Lisa A. Zuraff, "The National Park Service Winter Migration and Management Plan for American Elk in Rocky Mountain National Park," senior project paper, Colorado State University, Fort Collins (13 May 1988), 1. Also, on the seventy-fifth anniversary of Rocky Mountain National Park (3 August 1990), Thompson was interviewed by several Denver television stations. *The Denver Post* and the *Rocky Mountain News* published a number of articles on the park to mark the same anniversary. See Gary Gerhardt, "Parks Under Siege— Park Wildlife Pawns in Political Struggles," *Rocky Mountain News* (23 July 1991), 22.

28. Interviews with Stevens (January 1992) and McCutchen (June 1990).

29. During my vegetation and cover-type study in Rocky Mountain, I was continuously bombarded by questions from visitors. Those questions invariably focused on where elk could be found.

30. Catherine R. Berris, "Interactions of Elk and Residential Development: Planning, Design, and Attitudinal Considerations," *Landscape Journal* 6,1 (1987), 38–39.

31. Zuraff, "The National Park Service Winter Migration and Management Plan for American Elk in Rocky Mountain National Park," 1.

32. National Park Service, "Policy Statement," 1968. Emphases added.

33. January 1992 interview with Stevens. During the interview, Stevens

indicated that he was hoping to leave Rocky Mountain in the near future. He was actively searching for a new post. He believed that upon his departure from the park, he would be free to argue for the artificial reduction of the elk population there. Indeed, by the fall of 1991 Stevens had reluctantly reached the conclusion that artificial regulation of elk numbers was both necessary and inevitable in Rocky Mountain. Natural regulation was simply inadequate; the only question was whether artificial regulation should begin sooner or later. Stevens hoped to make his departing report on elk the forum for his recommendation.

34. Interviews with Stevens.

35. Ibid. Stevens stated that because Rocky Mountain was intended to be a preserve for nature and natural processes, he was reluctant to recommend artificial control of elk numbers.

36. The flaw in this reasoning should be apparent. Soil erosion and the loss of plant community and wildlife diversity are indeed "natural" responses to elk consuming huge quantities of willow, aspen, and grass. But the large population of elk foraging in Rocky Mountain is not natural; it is an artifact of human presence. Moreover, even if a case could be made for the naturalness of elk overgrazing, the question of its desirability would still remain. Certainly, Rocky Mountain was set aside as a monument to and reminder of nature. But the price for allowing elk to live "naturally" in the park is prohibitively high. In this case, it means devastation of land and life. To destroy nature in the name of preserving nature is a nonsensical strategy ill suited to a biosphere reserve.

37. Interview with Schoonveldt.

38. Stevens, "The Deer and Elk of Rocky Mountain National Park," 144.

39. Frederic H. Wagner, "Theory of Science's Role in Natural Resources and Environmental Policy—National Parks, A Case Study," paper presented at Conference on Business and the Environment: Applying Science to Environmental Policy in Canada and the United States (3–6 June 1989), Big Sky, Mont., Donner Foundation and the Foundation for Research on Economics and the Environment, 19.

40. David A. Bella, "Ethics and the Credibility of Applied Science" in U.S. Department of Agriculture, *Ethical Questions for Resource Managers,* U.S. Forest Service, Pacific Northwest Research Station General Technical Report PNW-GTR-288 (January 1992), 22.

41. Ibid., 26–27.

42. Interviews with Stevens and McCutchen (June 1990 and January 1992). McCutchen is the member of Rocky Mountain's science staff who has most consistently criticized natural regulation and has most often pronounced it a failure.

43. January 1991 interview with Stevens.

44. Thomas V. Skinner, "Background Data for Natural Fire Management in Rocky Mountain National Park," professional paper, Colorado State University, Fort Collins (November 1987), 5–7.

45. Ibid., 7–10; and interview with Laven. According to Skinner, Laven, and Park Service records, critical fire behavior and fire weather data, mandated by the 1972 forest plan, were never collected. The dramatic escalation of the fire after September 1 might not have occurred had park managers monitored (as they were required to) rate of fire speed, relative fire intensity, temperature, relative humidity, wind speed and direction, and fuel moisture. Although the park's decision to shelve the 1972 management plan was ostensibly made to avoid the risk of another Ouzel-type fire, it is also attributable to the park's failure to abide by the plan's strict fire control conditions. Risks cannot be avoided when natural fires are allowed to burn freely. However, the risks attending the Ouzel fire were needlessly expanded by Park Service negligence. The penalty for that negligence was borne entirely by the forests and wildlife of Rocky Mountain—a penalty extracted as the policy of fire suppression was instituted for yet another decade. Responsibility and accountability were once again diffused and carefully avoided.

46. Thomas V. Skinner and Richard D. Laven, "Background Data for Natural Fire Management in Rocky Mountain National Park—III," Grant No. Cx-1000-B-COXO, Department of Forest and Wood Sciences, Colorado State University, Fort Collins (31 March 1985), 37–40.

47. National Park Service, "Fire Management Plan for Rocky Mountain National Park, Colorado."

48. Ibid., 87. Emphasis in original.

49. Interview with Laven.

50. Interview with Craig Axtell, chief of resources management, Rocky Mountain National Park, Estes Park (25 March 1992).

51. Interviews with Axtell, Laven, and Mogren. Also see Skinner, "Background Data for Natural Fire Management in Rocky Mountain National Park" and Skinner and Laven, "Background Data for Natural Fire Management in Rocky Mountain National Park."

52. Interview with Axtell; and National Park Service, "Fire Management Plan for Rocky Mountain National Park Colorado."

53. Interview with Axtell.

54. Bruce M. Kilgore, "What *is Natural* in Wilderness Fire Management," in James E. Lotan, Bruce M. Kilgore, William C. Fisher, and Robert W. Mutch, eds., *Proceedings—Symposium and Workshop on Wilderness Fire*, U.S. Forest Service General Technical Report INT-182 (Washington, D.C.: Government Printing Office, 1985), 57.

55. Ibid., 63.

56. National Park Service, "Fire Management Plan for Rocky Mountain National Park, Colorado."

57. Interview with Laven.

58. Aldo Leopold, *A Sand County Almanac* (New York: Oxford University Press, 1949), 224–225.

59. Rolston, "Yellowstone: We Must Allow It to Change," 11–13.

60. Ethics provide guidance in determining what is good and bad and what constitutes moral duty and obligation. Aldo Leopold's land ethic, for example, attempts to deal with "man's relation to the land and to the animals and plants which grow upon it." His ethical dictum, "A thing is right when it tends to preserve the integrity, stability, and beauty of the biotic community . . . [and] wrong when it tends otherwise," is widely considered to be the yardstick by which the ecological rights and wrongs of human behavior can best be measured. Although many people consider Leopold's dictum to be profoundly ecological, its ethical content has little to do with the science of ecology. See Leopold, *A Sand County Almanac*, 203 and 224–225.

61. Responsible and accountable caretakers, those whose lives and careers are securely joined to the health of Rocky Mountain, must also be the arbiters of what constitutes the park's health. A healthy park can be defined in many different ways. Its health can be predicated on an historical reference point or defined in terms of biological diversity, sustainability, ecological functions, secure and adequate

boundaries, or the economic health of a larger landscape unit that includes neighboring human communities. Because no single definition of park health is intuitively correct, those who make the final decision must also be the ones who are responsible and accountable for making sure it comes about.

CHAPTER 5: RESTORING THE CROWN JEWEL

1. National Parks and Conservation Association, *A Race Against Time— Five Threats Endangering America's National Parks and the Solutions to Avert Them* (Washington, D.C.: NPCA, 20 August 1991).

2. Ibid., 9.

3. United States General Accounting Office, *Interior Issues,* GAO/OCG-89-24TR (Washington, D.C.: U.S. Government Printing Office, November 1988), 5.

4. T. Allan Comp, ed., *Blueprint for the Environment* (Salt Lake City: Howe Brothers, 1989). *Blueprint* was compiled through a cooperative effort of national environmental organizations. Among the book's many policy recommendations are increased appropriations to acquire new park lands, detailed and far-ranging studies of existing park boundaries, and greater protection of parks from external influences. Sadly, there is no recommendation that the National Park Service act more responsibly within the constraints of existing park boundaries and limited land resources.

5. *Rocky Mountain News,* 21 July 1991, 22–27 and 23 July 1991, 19–22.

6. *Rocky Mountain News,* 21 August 1991, 10.

7. *The Denver Post,* 29 April 1992, 10.

8. National Research Council, *Science and the National Parks* (Washington, D.C.: National Academy Press, 1992), 88.

9. Ibid., 108.

10. Ibid., 110–111.

11. Ibid., 110.

12. Michael Frome, *Regreening the National Parks* (Tucson: The University of Arizona Press, 1992), 231–232.

13. Information regarding Lorraine Mintzmyer was taken from Karl

Hess, "Former Park Official's Warning Comes Far Too Late," *Rocky Mountain News,* 12 October 1992; and interviews with National Park Service employees, unnamed by request.

14. See Joseph L. Sax, *Mountains Without Handrails* (Ann Arbor: The University of Michigan Press, 1980), 106–108.

15. Readers may object to my characterization of the National Park Service as a highly centralized bureaucracy. In some ways the Park Service is indeed decentralized. Many parks enjoy a surprising degree of operational autonomy, and many superintendents exercise almost total control over their respective parks. But such decentralization is only skin deep. When its facade of autonomy and self-rule is peeled away, institutional subservience and political uniformity are discovered. Superintendents are ultimately responsible for and accountable to an encompassing institutional body of bureaucratic logic and political constituencies that belies claims of independence. They function in an environment that bends their loyalties and wills away from the lands they oversee and toward more distant *and centralized* considerations of career advancement and political compliance. Decentralization of management over individual parks pales in comparison to the centralization of incentives and cues that so thoroughly affect the most crucial aspects of human behavior.

16. John Baden and Richard Stroup, "A Radical Proposal—Saving the Wilderness," *Reason* (July 1991), 28–36.

17. Part of the Trust's governing covenant would be public access, constrained only by admission fees and the ability of Rocky Mountain's ecosystem to safely support specific numbers of human visitors. In light of current visitation levels, higher fees would play a major role in keeping human numbers well within the park's carrying capacity. Low off-season fees would provide abundant opportunities for citizens with limited financial means to still access and enjoy the park.

18. One can only imagine the benefits that might be bestowed on America's crown jewels if the Conservation Trust were extended to every national park. Not only would the land and life of each park benefit as I hope Rocky Mountain will, but a diversity in management approaches to park protection would blossom from coast to coast. The uniform approaches imposed by centralized policy would give way to the reality of diversity. Ideas untried until now would

find fertile soil in which to test their efficacy and relevance. A richness of management options would emerge, offering ecologically sounder ways to protect and perpetuate America's most cherished landscapes.

19. Aldo Leopold, *A Sand County Almanac* (New York: Oxford University Press, 1949), 204.

20. The Conservation Trust embodies all of these tools and processes. It is a significant departure from the highly centralized Park Service. It is also an exercise in local democracy. In addition, membership shares in Rocky Mountain approximate the effects of and provide many of the benefits associated with private property ownership. Finally, free market forces, filling the vacuum left by the purging of national politics from Rocky Mountain, are crucial to the Trust's ability to survive, both economically and ecologically.

EPILOGUE

1. Karl Hess, "Former Park Official's Warning Comes Far Too Late," *Rocky Mountain News,* 12 October 1992.

2. James B. Thompson, superintendent, Rocky Mountain National Park, to Karl Hess, 23 October 1992.

3. David Stevens is now in Anchorage, Alaska, where he is still employed by the National Park Service.

4. At the time of publication of *Rocky Times in Rocky Mountain National Park,* the Park Service had begun advertising for the position of wildlife biologist at Rocky Mountain. Hopefully this book will persuade the park's administration to continue the work of Stevens and to take aggressive action to save the park's winter range.

5. Land reclamation scientists from Colorado State University have taken the lead in this project.

6. William A. Weber, *Colorado Flora: Eastern Slope* (Niwot: University Press of Colorado, 1990), 272. According to Weber, Rocky Mountain National Park has relied on the Turkish exotic grass *Festuca ovina* to reseed disturbed alpine roadsides instead of the native alpine grass *Festuca brachyphylla.* The variety of *Festuca ovina* used in Rocky Mountain is "covar."

7. Interview with National Park Service employee, 15 October 1992.

Index

United Nations UNESCO Man and
the Biosphere Program. *See*
Man and the Biosphere Program
University of Colorado, 13, 112
University of Wyoming, 30
University Press of Colorado, 117
Upslope fires, 58, 59–60, 62, 121
Urban impact. *See* Rocky Mountain
National Park, human impact
U.S. Fish and Wildlife Service, 27
U.S. Forest Service, 4
blue spruce management, 146(n79)
fire control, 55, 60
hunting and natural regulation, 24
tri-agency elk management project
(1960s), 20, 23
See also Roosevelt National Forest
U.S. Geological Survey, 108
Utah State University, 121

Values, 98, 99, 122
Vegetation conditions (elk winter
range)
inventory, *xiv*, 77
1930–1950, 28, 29
1950–1980s, 19, 22, 25, 26, 27, 28,
29, 83, 134(n61)
See also Aspen; Plant diversity; Exclosures; Grasslands; Meadows;
Understory vegetation; Willows
"Vision for the Future: A Framework
for Coordination in the Greater
Yellowstone Area" (NPS planning document), 106, 121
Visitation. *See* Tourism

Wagner, Frederic, 90
Water degradation, 27
Water table, 11, 48
dams maintaining, 46(photo), 47
Weeds, 10, 16, 18, 38, 39, 48

Western spruce budworm, 10, 60, 66,
67, 68, 93
Wetlands, 27, 47, 49, 72, 73, 80, 119
acquisition, 117–118
riparian, 11–12(photos), 27
See also Meadows
White River National Forest,
145(n78)
Wild Basin, 65(photo), 72
Wilderness system, 6, 111
Wildflowers, 61, 62, 63, 68
Wildlife habitat, 3, 66
disappearance, 62
Willows, 6
alpine/subalpine, 39, 43
and beaver, 45, 47
carr acquisition, 118
in exclosures, 29, 35(photos)
field reports (1975–1990), 38–39
grazed/hedged, 10, 11, 12, 18, 21,
28–29, 33, 35–36(photos), 38,
39, 45, 46, 48, 75
and water table, 47, 48
Wind Cave National Park, 121
Winds, 57, 58
Windy Gulch, 120
Winter range (elk), 16–17, 20, 48,
54, 77, 84, 85, 91, 92
area of, 16–17, 21, 39, 43, 129(n22)
and bighorn sheep, 43
fire frequency, 58
migration disruption in, 82, 102
reports (1930–1990), 17, 18, 19, 26
tri-agency elk management project
(1960s), 21
See also Carrying capacity; Soil, erosion; Vegetation conditions
Wolves, 2, 3, 22, 48, 81, 82, 84, 121
Woodlands
open pine, 53, 54, 68, 69, 70
Wyoming
aspen study, 30

LOVE
from Sesame Street

By Sesame Workshop
Illustrated by Ernie Kwiat

LOVE is a

2